Shemuel Hanagid

ASHER LEHMANN

Shemuel Hanagid

Translated by *Sheindel Weinbach*

FELDHEIM PUBLISHERS ✦ *Jerusalem / New York*

Edited by Karen Paritzky and Uri Kaploun

First published 1980
ISBN 0-87306-220-5

Copyright © 1980 by
Feldheim Publishers Ltd

All rights reserved

No part of this publication may be translated,
reproduced, stored in a retrieval system or transmitted,
in any form or by any means,
electronic, mechanical, photocopying, recording or otherwise,
without prior permission in writing from the publishers

Phototypeset at the Feldheim Press

Philipp Feldheim Inc.
96 East Broadway
New York, NY 10002

Feldheim Publishers Ltd
POB 6525 / Jerusalem, Israel

Printed in Israel

Dedicated

in memory of

REUBEN GREVNIN

by his wife, daughter and family

ראובן בן שלמה יצחק
נלב״ע כ״ז שבט תשל״ח
והוטמן בהר המנוחות, ירושלים
ת נ צ ב ״ ה

This edition has been supported in part
by a grant from
Yaïr Publications
Jerusalem

contents

1 Cordoba ~ 9
2 The Academies of Babylonia ~ 13
3 Act of God ~ 17
4 Shemuel ben Yosef ~ 24
5 The Royal Scribe ~ 40
6 Granada ~ 44
7 Kidnap and Ransom ~ 46
8 A Sage in Bondage ~ 53
9 The Ruler and the Rabbi ~ 57
10 The Power of the Pen ~ 64
11 By the Waters of Babylon ~ 72
12 The Peerless Vizier ~ 83
13 An Assassin Strikes ~ 86
14 A Tongue for a Tongue ~ 90
15 From Bondage to Freedom ~ 96
16 A Suitable Match ~ 99
17 An Unexpected Wedding Guest ~ 107
18 The Mitzvah Feast ~ 113
19 A Title of Esteem ~ 118
20 Yehosef ben Shemuel ~ 123

21	The Young Poet's Visit ∽ *128*
22	Plots and Plotters ∽ *133*
23	More Plots and More Plotters ∽ *136*
24	Consultation at Midnight ∽ *141*
25	The Contest for the Throne ∽ *148*
26	A Political Parable ∽ *151*
27	The Power of Reproof ∽ *154*
28	Rav Nissim and his Disciple ∽ *158*
29	Prideful Provocation ∽ *162*
30	Ambush in the Mountains ∽ *167*
31	The Disputation ∽ *174*
32	Islam or the Sword ∽ *181*
33	Poetic Pranks ∽ *190*
34	Preparing for the End ∽ *198*

Glossary ∽ *205*

1 Cordoba

Have you, dear reader, ever visited the country in which the fugitives of Israel found a haven after the destruction of the *beith hamikdash*, the Holy Temple in Jerusalem, and where they rose to unequalled heights? Are you familiar with that land in which your brethren held positions as ministers and your ancestors excelled in diplomacy, administering the affairs of nations? If not, then escape with me from our turbulent present to the distant past, to a place where Semites ruled, and chose God-fearing, Torah-observant Jews as their ministers and advisers. Let us shake off the dust of our times and escape to the shade of cypress glades, to long, myrtle-lined avenues, and to the banks of streams, where one can almost hear the whispering of the colorful wings of the butterfly, where the soul can refresh itself with pleasant dreams and savor *Gan Eiden* (Paradise). We will bring to life before our mind's eye some of the richest scenes of our past, crowded with the noble figures of ministers and councilors who were renowned for their Torah scholarship, as well as for their poetry praising Hashem in the holy tongue.

[*Shemuel Hanagid*

In a southern region of Spain known as Sierra de Cordoba, on the right bank of the great Guadalquivir River, there lies an ancient city, surrounded by picturesque walls studded with turrets and towers. This is the city of Cordoba, inhabited by a Jewish community as far back as the Talmudic era, as we may see from an incident involving Spain mentioned in the Talmud (*Yevamoth* 115), in which it is reported that Yitzchak the Exilarch once visited *Cortaba*. Today, Cordoba is a medium-sized city with only minor industry and underdeveloped trade. In the period of this story, however (around the year 4760 — 1000 C.E.), it was at the peak of its development and brilliance, being the capital of the Caliphate Empire founded in A.M. 4515 (755 C.E.) by Abd-el-Rahman the First. Cordoba grew by leaps and bounds and, within a short time, became the most highly developed and thriving city of the Iberian Peninsula. The area covered by the city was so vast that it took six hours to walk around it. With its one million inhabitants, it boasted 600 mosques, 60,000 buildings of grand proportions, 900 public baths, a distinguished university with (for those times) a huge library comprising 600 manuscripts written on smooth lamb's parchment, and eighty public schools.

The royal palace was built in legendary splendor: the main palace, Atzara, rested on 4,300 gold-based marble pillars. Of no lesser grandeur were the various harems and buildings adjoining it.

Cordoba was, at the same time, also a center of poetry, art, and science. Even the rulers of Florence in Italy could not boast of such vast collections of rare works of art, of rich libraries with as many precious manuscripts, and of as many residences for scholars, scientists, and philosophers as could Cordoba. The city teemed with wise men and scribes, and even its rulers dabbled in poetry and science. Teachers and students alike streamed there from Christian lands as well as from the Moslem world. In fact, the Moslems who ruled Spain in those times regarded it as a holy city.

The Jewish community benefited greatly from the blossoming prosperity of the city. While the majority lived in the narrow streets at the foot of the mountain or in the towers of the city walls, many Jews resided in grand palaces, whose ornate and graceful arches were embellished by the most fashionable Moorish artisans. Others maintained summer homes in the Secunda suburb, in whose carefully groomed gardens orange trees released their fragrance and whose water fountains refreshed the air.

Torah study flourished in that golden era of Cordoba, or, as the Phoenicians had originally named it, *Karta-Tava*, which in Aramaic means "the Good City." Here resided the famous grammarian Rabbi Yehudah Chiyuj, towards whom disciples converged from all over the world to study the grammar of the holy tongue, and here lived many great Jewish poets. These Torah scholars also pursued those secular

[*Shemuel Hanagid*

subjects needed to perfect their Torah knowledge, especially medicine, mathematics, and astronomy.

This pre-eminence of Cordoba as a center of Torah learning derived from the personality of its *rosh yeshivah* (head of the Torah academy), Rabbeinu Chanoch ben Mosheh, who had arrived there some fifty years before the time of our story, by a singular act of Providence.

*The street of the Jews in Cordoba.
According to local tradition, the building shown
was the birthplace of Rambam (Maimonides).*

2 the academies of Babylonia

The most significant Torah center outside of *Eretz Yisrael* was situated in the land of Babylonia. Even prior to the destruction of the first beith hamikdash, the artisans — the *charash* and the *masger* mentioned in the Biblical record of the period (*Melachim* 24:14) — were exiled there together with King Yechonyah. According to a tradition of our Sages, these were the greatest Torah scholars, "whose listeners turned dumb (*cheresh*) when they opened their mouths to lecture, and whose profound questions produced a deadlock (*masger*=locksmith) for there was no one who could answer." Our Sages also explain that this elite was exiled first in order to prevent the Torah from being forgotten, God forbid. Thus it was that by the time of the destruction of the beith hamikdash, when so many scholars and their disciples were killed and the yeshivoth of Eretz Yisrael were silenced, the exiles had been living in peace in Babylonia for several years and had founded a number of great yeshivoth. From then on, Torah study flourished in Babylonia, even in the time of the second beith hamikdash, and beyond.

This was especially so when the great *amora*

(Talmudic sage) Abba Aricha settled in Babylonia after the destruction of the second beith hamikdash and established his yeshivah in the city of Sura. Rav (as Abba Aricha was generally called) invested all his energies in propagating Torah knowledge among Jews. His choice of Sura as the city in which to establish a Torah center is based on an interesting story. He once heard a woman ask her friend, "How much milk do you need in order to cook half a pound of meat?" Upon hearing that ignorance was so rampant that Jewish women did not know the explicit commandment of the Torah prohibiting the cooking of meat with milk, he was shaken to the core and decided to found a yeshivah in the very place where Torah knowledge had sunk so low. And, indeed, the famous academy he established in Sura drew many thousands of students. From that time on, Sura and Neharda'a — where his colleague Mar Shemuel had his yeshivah — became the main Torah centers, although learning also flourished in other places, such as Pumbaditha and Matha-Mechasya.

At the time when Christianity was gaining ascendancy, and the *Yishuv* (Jewish community in the land of Israel) was dispersed and destroyed, the yeshivoth in Babylonia remained the sole Torah centers in the world. It was there that the editing of the Talmud was completed by Ravina and Rav Ashi, and it was there that their successors, the *rabbanan sevora'ey*, added their commentaries and halachic decisions to the

The Academies of Babylonia]

Talmud. Even in the succeeding period of the *geonim* (the roshey yeshivah in Babylonia), this country continued to serve as the Torah center of the world. Although Jewry was dispersed more and more among the nations, no major yeshivah was established elsewhere.

The scholars of the Babylonian yeshivoth received queries from all over the world in all areas of the Torah — requests for halachic decisions, and for the elucidation of difficult legal and aggadic passages in the Talmud. The Babylonian scholars replied to all these queries, and some of their responsa are preserved to this day. Several of the geonim compiled their responsa and wrote commentaries on selected texts, but there was no comprehensive commentary on the Talmud such as that of Rashi, nor any codified halachic work resembling the *Mishneh Torah* of Rabbeinu Mosheh ben Maimon (otherwise known as Rambam, or Maimonides). There was therefore no way of excelling in Torah learning except by studying the entire Talmud with an expert rabbi and hearing his oral commentary, and this was possible almost solely in the Babylonian yeshivoth.

Babylonia, however, did not escape hard times. During the period of Rav Chaninai, the Gaon of Sura, Rav Chana, the Gaon of Pumbaditha, and Mar Rav Yitzchak, the Gaon of Piruz Shapur, the country was captured by the Arabs. In order to incline the new ruler favorably towards the Jews, Mar Rav Yitzchak Gaon went forth to greet the conqueror, Ali ibn Abu T'aleb, who graciously acknowledged the gesture. And indeed, at first the Arab conquest brought them respite from the evil decrees and persecution that marked the end of Persian rule. Later, however, the attitude of the Arab government changed toward the Jews. Instead of the almost unlimited autonomy they had been granted at first — the exilarch, a descendant of King David, was their officially recognized ruler, and the geonim held judicial powers over the Jewish community — now many rights were denied them and their situation deteriorated drastically.

3
Act of God

In the course of time, the Arab government had made it a practice to *sell* the office of exilarch to the highest bidder, and this opened the door for unscrupulous, grasping men to gain power over the Jewish community. Since the new exilarchs did not always submit to the Torah authority of the geonim, this state of affairs caused dissension and resulted not only in a marked decline of Torah study in Babylon, but held dangerous prospects for Judaism as a whole. One Jew, named Anan, who aspired to the post of exilarch but did not receive the approval of the geonim, sought to avenge himself by founding a new sect — the Karaites. This sect, similar to the *Tzedukim* (Sadducees) at the time of the second beith hamikdash, adhered only to the Written Torah and denied the authoritativeness of the tradition of the Sages as recorded in the *Mishnah* and *Gemara* (which together constitute the Oral Torah).

Just before the end of this epoch, however, two geonim arose who surpassed even their predecessors in wisdom: Rav Sherira Gaon and his son, Rav Hai Gaon. When Rav Sherira saw that his son was suited to lead the community, he appointed him *av beith din* (head of the rabbinical court). Rav Hai Gaon disseminated Torah to such an extent that it was said that he had no equal among the geonim. He was descended from King David through Zerubavel ben Shealtiel: his insignia was a lion. His end, however, was swift and bitter, for an Arab king imprisoned him and his father, confiscated all their property, and eventually hanged Rav Sherira by one hand when this venerable sage was one hundred years old. According to the Ari z"l, this calamity is hinted at in the verse in *Eichah*: "*Sarim* (Sherira) *beyadam nithlu* — Ministers were hanged by their hand." Shortly afterwards, with the death of his son, Rav Hai Gaon, the period of the geonim in Babylonia ended. But even during Rav Sherira's lifetime Divine Providence prepared the way for Torah wisdom, especially knowledge of the Talmud, to spread to all corners of the world.

The spiritual deterioration of the Babylonian Jewish community was accompanied by the material decline of its yeshivoth. Since they constituted the Torah center of the entire world, they received funds from all the Jewish communities of the diaspora, especially from Spain, West and North Africa, Egypt and Eretz Yisrael. Now, in view of a most difficult situation, the roshey yeshivah decided to send four sages to these communities in order to collect donations and pledges to maintain their academies. The people taking part in this undertaking were: Rabbeinu

Act of God]

Chushiel; Rabbeinu Mosheh ben Chanoch, accompanied by his wife and his infant son Chanoch; Rabbeinu Shemaryahu ben Rabbi Elchanan; and a fourth whose name is not recorded by history.

On the high seas their ship was attacked by the notorious band of pirates led by ibn-Damahin, agent of the Arab king in Spain, Abd-el-Rahman el-Nasr. This pirate king's net was spread over the length and breadth of the Mediterranean Sea from Italy to Eretz Yisrael, and the four scholars were captured just off the Italian coast. When the brigand chief set eyes upon Rabbeinu Mosheh ben Chanoch's beautiful wife, he plotted to capture her. Sensing the imminent danger, the young woman asked her husband in Hebrew if people who meet their death by drowning rise for *techiyyath hameithim* (the resurrection of the dead). Her husband answered her with the verse from Psalms (68:23): "Hashem says, 'From Bashan I will return them, I will return them from the depths of the sea.'" Upon hearing these words she flung herself into the sea — like the four hundred boys and girls we read of in the Talmud (*Gittin* 57b).

Thanks to a gracious Providence, these scholars were sold by their captors in widely separated places, thus allowing the Torah to be disseminated in many lands. Rabbeinu Shemaryahu was sold in Alexandria, on the coast of Egypt, where the local Jews redeemed him and established him as their rosh yeshivah. Rabbeinu Chushiel was sold in Africa and became a

[Shemuel Hanagid

rosh yeshivah in Kairwan, the greatest fortified city of the Arab empire in North Africa. His son, Rabbeinu Chananel, who was later born there, was to become the renowned Talmudic commentator whose Torah-waters nourished all the *rishonim*, as the early medieval authorities were called. Rabbeinu Mosheh and his son Chanoch were brought to Cordoba by their brigand captors. Even though they did not reveal their identity, they were redeemed by the Jews of the city, for Jews have always excelled in the mitzvah of *pidyon shevuyim*, the ransoming of captives.

In those days there was a large *beith midrash* (study house) in Cordoba, known as Keneseth Hamidrash, in which the *dayyan* (judge) of the Jewish community, Rabbi Nathan Chasid, expounded Torah to his disciples, explaining it to the best of his knowledge. This is the place to which Rabbeinu Mosheh and his son Chanoch headed immediately upon their release. That day the subject of study was the *avodah* (Divine service) of the *kohein gadol* (high priest) on Yom Kippur, as described in the Talmudic tractate *Yoma*. They were discussing the rule stating: "For every sprinkling — an immersion," that is, when the high priest entered the Holy of Holies, he was required to dip his finger into the vessel containing the sacrificial blood before each time he sprinkled it near the Ark of the Covenant [*Tosefta Yoma* 3:2]. But Rabbi Nathan incorrectly explained the rule to mean that the high priest was required to immerse himself in a *mikveh* (ritual bath) before each sprinkling. Rabbeinu Mosheh, who until now had been sitting in a corner dressed in a simple sackcloth garment, arose and asked, "If this is the meaning, then the high priest would have had to immerse himself many more times than the five mentioned in the Mishnah (*Yoma* 3:3), for there were many more than five sprinklings!"

His words caused general amazement in the beith midrash. The newly-redeemed stranger suddenly revealed himself as an erudite Talmudic scholar as he began to explain the tosefta correctly. He was quickly surrounded by the students in the beith midrash, all plying him with questions on topics in the Talmud. Rabbeinu Mosheh was able to answer them all.

Until that day Rabbi Nathan Chasid had been accustomed to remain all day in the beith midrash after he had finished his lecture in order to judge the various litigants who came to present their cases. This time, however, he prepared to leave the beith midrash with his students immediately upon finishing his lecture, paying no attention to the litigants who awaited him. These, however, quickly followed him, requesting an explanation. Rabbi Nathan turned to them and, in full humility, replied, "I am no longer permitted to be your judge. The man who has entered our beith midrash today, dressed in sackcloth, is a greater scholar than I am — he must be your judge from now on. He is the master and I am his disciple."

These words, said in all seriousness, were accepted

with the same seriousness. The community of Cordoba appointed Rabbeinu Mosheh as its judge and rosh yeshivah and, in keeping with these honorable offices, clothed him fittingly, put a carriage at his disposal, and accorded him a handsome salary. When the pirate saw the treasure he had disposed of at such a cheap price, he regretted the sale, kidnapped Rabbeinu Mosheh again, and demanded a huge ransom. The Jewish community appealed to the king in an urgent demand for justice. At the same time, they made a point of explaining the political benefit that would accrue to him if the Jews of Spain ceased being dependent on their brethren in Babylonia. They stressed that through Rabbeinu Mosheh's yeshivah, Cordoba would become a Torah center for all of Europe and North Africa, a situation that would also bring considerable financial benefits. The petition bore the desired fruit, and a governmental decree ordered his release.

Spain had been inhabited by Jews from as far back as the destruction of the Temple in Jerusalem in the first century C.E. As Rambam testifies, he himself was descended from a Spanish family that had fled from Jerusalem to Spain. In Germany and France, too, there were ancient Jewish communities which had handed Torah down from generation to generation — as Rabbeinu Asher testifies in his responsa — from the time of the destruction of the Temple. Interesting evidence of the antiquity of the Jewish community of Mayence in Germany was unearthed in the local cemetery in the time of the Maharil (ca. 5150 — 1390 C.E.): the tombstone of a *shifchah charufah* (a betrothed Jewish bondmaid; see *Vayikra* 19:20) dating back one thousand years. Throughout this time, these diaspora communities had always considered the yeshivoth of Babylonia their spiritual center. Now, however, the situation underwent a basic change. The presence of one of the foremost Babylonian scholars in Spain transformed the country, and particularly Cordoba, into a new Torah center.

After Rabbeinu Mosheh's death Rabbeinu Chanoch succeeded his father, and with his disciples a new era in Jewish history began: the period of the *rabbanim*.

4 Shemuel ben Yosef

These were the days of the great Spanish caliph, Abd-el-Rahman, whose prime minister was one of Judaism's outstanding personalities: Rabbi Chasdai ibn Shaprut. Rabbi Chasdai was the recognized leader of Spanish Jewry who gave him the title of *Nasi*, which means prince.

Abd-el-Rahman was anxious to establish Cordoba as an independent spiritual center for the Jewish community, and he gave Chasdai his wholehearted support to foster the development of the new yeshivah, headed by Rabbi Mosheh ben Chanoch. News of this new academy spread rapidly from country to country and Jewish scholars streamed to Cordoba from all over the world.

This period also saw an intensified interest in the study of Hebrew grammar. The Hebrew language scholar, Menachem ben Saruk compiled a large dictionary, called *Machbereth*. His system, however, was challenged by another grammarian, Dunash ibn Labrat, who had come to Cordoba from the city of Fez. Their difference of opinion agitated all the learned Jews of the community. In short, this was a period of

Shemuel ben Yosef]

vigorous, pulsating Jewish intellectual and spiritual activity.

At this time, a certain Jew, Yosef Halevi, tanner of delicate parchments, lived in the small Spanish town of Merida, on the northern bank of the Guadiana River. A scholar of Jewish studies in his own right, he had long wanted to join the learned community of Cordoba and when anti-Jewish pogroms broke out in his birthplace, he and his wife fled there.

The craft of tanning delicate parchment was flourishing in Cordoba, especially among Jews who had modernized the process considerably. Rabbi Yosef was an expert craftsman, and he hoped now to improve his financial status. The southern bank of the river had many workshop-huts where the tanners plied their craft. Rabbi Yosef also set up such a hut, and within a short time he gained many customers for his fine parchment, which was perfect for binding books.

His financial situation improved greatly and he would have been happy with his lot — were it not for the lack of one thing. Hashem *yithbarach* had denied him children. One day his righteous, gracious wife complained about it, and he comforted her with the words of Elkanah, father of the prophet Shemuel, "Why do you weep, and why do you not eat, and why is your heart troubled? Am I not better to you than ten sons?"

And she, too, replied in words similar to those of Elkanah's wife, Channah: "If Hashem will see the suffering of his maidservant and give her a son, he will be the servant of God and a shield and savior for his brethren."

In fact, Yosef's family stemmed, like that of the prophet Shemuel, from the families of the sons of Korach.

It was not long after this conversation that Yosef's wife bore a fine healthy son, in the year 4753 (993 C.E.) and, in keeping with her words, she named him Shemuel.

Rabbi Yosef and his wife tried with all their might to educate their only son to Torah and piety, and these efforts were crowned with success. Whoever saw the young boy would recall the verse of the book of *Mishley* (Proverbs 20:11), "Even in his rompings is a youth recognized, if he be pure and if his deeds are honest."

Shemuel had no taste for the games of children of his age, for his mental abilities were developed to an extraordinary extent and he strove for more elevated goals. The serenity of *yir'ath shamayim* (the fear of Heaven) radiated from his pleasant face. During his prayers he stood quietly in his place and prayed with the intensity of an adult, as if he had inherited from his ancestress Channah the quality of her prayer — "Only her lips moved and her voice could not be heard." At a very early age he had already mastered all of *Chummash* (Five Books of Moses) with its musical notes. At ten he was counted among the most gifted students of the rosh yeshivah, Rabbeinu Chanoch, who was convinced that this lad had been born to greatness.

With reference to Shemuel he used to quote the saying of Rabbi Chanina, "I have learned much from my teachers, more from my colleagues, but most of all from my pupils" (*Ta'anith* 7a). Shemuel studied Hebrew grammar under Rabbi Yehudah Chiyuj, excelling in this study as in all others. Later he began to study the secular subjects necessary to complete his Torah knowledge, and soon became expert in astronomy and medicine, arousing the amazement of his Arab teachers. A noted Arab astronomer once told him in his youth: "A student who has a good memory without a spirit of understanding and creativity is no more than a donkey carrying books. But you, Shemuel my son, have the power of a mighty horse, blessed with all these exalted characteristics alike."

As Shemuel grew up, he appeared to all as one destined for greatness, favored by God and man. He was now faced with the question of which profession he should choose. He did not want to earn a living from his knowledge of Torah, but sought a means of livelihood as our Sages advised, "a clean and simple craft," so that he would be free to pursue Torah study during most of the hours of the day, leaving his work as an occupation of secondary importance. In the end he decided to open a grocery store, an undertaking which did not require too great a financial investment. In the store he opened a pharmacy section—a novelty for Spain at this time, since pharmacy was connected with the medical profession, and doctors were also druggists.

[Shemuel Hanagid

One of the Arab scholars in Cordoba had recommended that pharmaceutics be separated from medicine and, indeed, there were already several peddlers who sold simple medicines. However, complex prescriptions combining several ingredients were available only through doctors. One of Rabbi Shemuel's friends, Rabbi Yonah ibn Janach, who became a major influence in his life, had written a book in Latin on medicines and the measurements and weights of their formulas. Rabbi Shemuel decided to open his pharmacy, the first of its kind, dispensing prescriptions based on this work. Though still considered a peddler, he was really Spain's first pharmacist.

Rabbi Shemuel set fixed prices for every commodity and refused to waste his time bargaining with customers, as was the rule in all other shops. If his customer did not agree to the fixed price, Rabbi Shmuel would leave the transaction and return to his studying. This practice brought him double profit: first, from the precious time not wasted on idle haggling and, secondly, he won himself a name as an honest and trustworthy merchant. As a result, customers began to stream to his store, about which he used to say, "Probably Satan is bothered by my involvement in Torah, so he sends me so many customers; he is not interested in distracting other merchants—who do not study Torah—from their idle pursuits, and so he does not send them so many."

He thus enjoyed some years of peace and contentment, supporting himself from his shop and progressing in his pursuit of Torah and wisdom. But one day the skies of Cordoba suddenly darkened; catastrophic events shook the firm position of the community and of Rabbi Shemuel alike, and disaster quickly overtook him.

The caliph of Cordoba, Hisham the Second, was a fickle, weak ruler. His predecessor had been deposed after a revolt by Slavic soldiers who had set Hisham on the throne, but he was completely dependent on their will. In Cordoba itself he had many enemies and dissenters. When the internal conflicts between the Cordobans and the Slavs reached their peak, the Omayyads, who refused to suffer the rule of the caliph's Slavic officers, appealed to Suleiman, caliph of the Berbers, and informed him that they were ready to turn the city over to him if he approached the city gates at a specified time.

Thus it was that on the sixth day of Iyar, 4773 (1013 C.E.), in the midst of heavy internal struggle, the city gates suddenly opened, and Berber troops swept into the city through the suburbs of Secunda, whose gate had been opened to them by a bribed officer.

When the Slavs were convinced that they no longer had the upper hand, they retreated, and the Berbers (called "Philistines" by the Jews) began to plunder and murder, unleashing their wrath mainly on the defenseless Jews. That day was a bitter one for the

[Shemuel Hanagid

Jewish community of Cordoba. The crown of the Torah was trampled in the dust and Jewish leaders were cruelly murdered. On that day the venerable Rabbi Yitzchak, the wise and righteous judge, was killed, as was Rabbi Shalom ben Duriyad, the author of a Talmudic dictionary. Another who died on that day sanctifying Hashem's name was Rabbi Yehudah ben Yosef ben Chasdai, renowned for his knowledge of astronomy and medicine. Finally, after the plunder and massacre, the vandals burned the entire city so as not to leave a trace of the inhabitants' property.

On the day following the capture of the city, Suleiman seized the palace of Caliph Hisham. In spite of the depression and despair they felt, all the Cordobans who had survived were forced to cry, "Long live the Caliph!" as Suleiman entered the palace. He himself understood full well the value of this artificial fervor, and described the event in the grisly doggerel of a well-known poet:

> They smile, and shout "Long life!"
> But wish me woe and strife;
> My face they claim to like —
> Best seen atop a pike ...

At first Suleiman and his Berbers occupied only the Secunda suburb, but very soon all of the remaining Cordobans were forced to leave the city, and their property was confiscated by the conquerors. Among the exiles was Rabbi Shemuel: bereft of everything, he had to flee for his life. Already he had lost his parents — he had searched for them in vain ever since the massacre on the day the city was captured, so he had no choice but to believe that they had been killed by the vandals or had perished in the great fire.

He wandered in the field, solitary, not knowing where to turn or where to go. Reaching a small wood, he decided to rest awhile until his strength returned. He entered the shade of the trees and poured out his sore heart before the Master of the world.

"How enviable is the lot of those who died sanctifying Your Name!" he murmured. "Their souls repose in the holiness of eternal life. Why did I not merit to die such a death in order to enjoy the light of the *Shechinah* (divine Presence) together with the righteous in Gan Eiden, instead of having to contend with suffering, and the difficult trials of life?"

His prayers came from his lips easily, and in this Rabbi Shemuel found solace, for according to the tradition of our rabbis, this is a clear sign that one's prayers are being accepted favorably. The encouraging thought came to him that, since it had been decreed by Providence that he remain alive, this must be so because significant tasks were awaiting him. Though aware of the fact that he was blessed with rare talents, he was a humble person, and never dared to speak before anyone wiser or older than he. Seeing, however, that greater and better people than he had been martyred while he had been spared, he decided that, although he was not yet of venerable age, it was his sacred duty to teach Torah to others, to disseminate the knowledge he had received from his great teacher, Rabbeinu Chanoch, and to utilize the gifts with which Hashem had blessed him, to the advantage of his fellow Jews.

He recalled the words of his father, who when he was a boy had always encouraged him to study Torah saying, "Shemuel, my son, study Torah diligently and steadily, for a man can own no lasting possessions save for the wisdom he has learned." His father used to repeat the words of the Midrash of Rabbi Tanchuma (*parashath Yithro*):

> A *talmid chacham* (scholar) was traveling in a ship full of merchants. Whenever they asked him where his merchandise was he would reply, "My goods are more valuable than yours." They searched the entire ship but found nothing, and began to mock him. In mid-journey a band of pirates attacked the ship, plundering everything aboard it. The survivors reached land and found themselves in a strange country, bereft of all their possessions. What did the talmid chacham do? He entered a beith midrash and began to teach. When the people there saw that he was a Torah scholar they received him respectfully and appointed him as their rabbi, rewarding him with a handsome salary. Wherever he went, the members of the congregation would accompany

him. One day, the stranded merchants met him with his respectful companions and approached him, saying: "We beg of you, please speak on our behalf to the people of the city, if only for some food to sustain us, for you know what we were and what we had aboard ship." And, agreeing to their request, he replied, "Did I not tell you that my wares are more valuable than yours?"

This *midrash* (rabbinic story) reminded Rabbi Shemuel of the capture and ransom of Rabbeinu Mosheh, the father of his teacher, Rabbi Chanoch, who had used his wares to give the world a new Torah center.

"Surely," he thought, "now that Hashem has kept me alive, I must dedicate my life to serve Him, and work to the best of my ability to alleviate the suffering of the Jewish people."

At that moment, Rabbi Shemuel recalled that when the Berbers had attacked his street, killing and plundering, he had hurriedly hidden a gold ring set with a precious stone inside the lining of his shoe. The devastating events that had followed had made him forget it completely. He quickly took off his shoe: the precious ring was in its place! His eyes lit up. He was no longer the penniless pauper he had thought he was. He recalled the verse: "Before they call I will answer," and thanked Hashem for having heard his prayer — for having prepared, in the metaphor of the Sages, the "remedy before the ailment." He would head for Malaga, and try to pawn his ring in order to open a small shop. Malaga, being a port city, was constantly visited by wealthy merchants. It should not be too difficult to get a good price for a ring with a precious gem.

Where today the Malaga-Cordoba railroad runs, there lay, at the time of our story, a pedestrian road which had of late been neglected and left in a state of disrepair. The Berber armies, stationed in that area for the past several years in order to stage their battles on Cordoba, had destroyed the still-usable remains of the road, so that people who ventured to use it would occasionally have to plow through mud above their knees.

On this long and tedious road, Rabbi Shemuel reviewed by heart some chapters of Mishnah, as he was accustomed to do whenever he was unable to study intensively. He discovered that despite his suffering and hardship, he had fortunately not forgotten his learning, and the *mishnayoth* (paragraphs of the Mishnah) still came easily to his lips. Alone on a lonely road, he truly felt what King David had felt before him (*Tehillim* 119:92): "Were not Your Torah my recreation, I would have perished in my affliction."

Keeping his eyes on the road, he proceeded on his way. On the second day of his journey, he suddenly noticed two outlines on the horizon — two Jews, perhaps, who were likewise traveling to Malaga...? He quickened his steps and, as he peered ahead, it seemed to him that one of them ... could it be ... his brother ... Rabbi Yitzchak? He called out to the wayfarers, and Rabbi Yitzchak — for indeed it was he — turning his head, immediately recognized his brother. Overcome by emotion, the two brothers embraced wordlessly.

"Do you know anything about the whereabouts of Father and Mother?" was Rabbi Shemuel's first question.

"To my sorrow, I know nothing about them," replied Rabbi Yitzchak sadly.

His traveling companion was also a close acquaintance of Rabbi Shemuel's, the same Rabbi Yonah ibn Janach whose medical prescriptions Rabbi Shemuel used to dispense in happier times. The three now continued together on the road to Malaga.

The emotion evoked by the surprise meeting stirred Rabbi Shemuel's poetic Muse, for it was always his habit, upon any happy or sad event in his life, to compose poetry in the language of the Torah. The three poems that he composed in the wake of leaving Cordoba are preserved to this day in his book, *Ben Tehillim*.

The southward tramp along the gutted road had taken many days, and had exhausted the strength of the three travelers. But one fine day they finally saw from afar a lovely port city nestling near the harbor on the Mediterranean Sea. They were already nearing the banks of the Guadalmedina River which, several miles before reaching the city, widens immensely. They climbed up the steep Gibralpere Mountain overlooking Malaga, from whose peak a fortress frowned.

From the mountain top they looked down upon the harbor and the city, marveling at the magnificent scenery which spread out before their eyes. Rabbi Shemuel pronounced the blessing upon seeing the sea, "*Oseh ma'aseh bereishith*," (praising Him Who wrought the work of Creation), and his two companions answered "Amen." However, his brother Rabbi Yitzchak commented that according to his view, he should have recited a different blessing, "*She'asah hayam hagadol*" (Who made the great sea).

The two brothers thus continued to discuss the *halachah* (Torah law), temporarily forgetting their sorrow and anguish. They rejoiced especially that after such a long lapse they were able once more to sharpen their wits on scholarly topics.

Vegetable gardens with rows of carefully tended flowers showed the travelers that they were nearing the city. However, once they entered the city gates the contrast within clearly defined itself. It appeared as if the residents had purposely neglected their city and had intended it to be ugly. Crooked streets full of filth and stench bore witness that this was a port city. The streets and houses, devoid of any beauty, appeared to have been set down in haphazard fashion. Before almost every house there stood sacks and vessels of raisins, wine, olive oil, almonds, and the like. Sailors and dockworkers hastened to and fro, occupied with their pursuits.

Rabbi Shemuel and his companions passed through the dank streets and narrow alleys until they reached the large market square. Suddenly they opened their eyes wide. Who was that coming towards them? Did he not truly resemble one of their dearest friends from Cordoba? Surely! It was none other than the merchant, Rabbi Yehudah ibn Gabirol.

When Rabbi Yehudah recognized the three men coming toward him he was overcome with emotion and, out of the fullness of his heart, recited the blessing "*Mechayyeh hameithim*," in praise of the One Who resurrects the dead. He inquired about the welfare of all his acquaintances and friends in Cordoba and related how he and his wife had been rescued from the vandals there. A gentile acquaintance had taken them — for a handsome fee, to be sure — on speedy camels and had brought them swiftly to the banks of the Guadalmedina River. There they had embarked on a boat that brought them to Malaga.

Rabbi Yehudah ibn Gabirol, known to the Arabs as Iyov ibn Yichye, had succeeded in saving most of his fortune. He was a merchant of precious gems and pearls, and when the riots began in Cordoba he had hastily hidden his wares inside his clothes. Upon arriving in Malaga he had opened a jewelry store which soon began to thrive.

[Shemuel Hanagid

It was fortunate for Rabbi Shemuel to have met a trusted friend who was an expert in precious stones. On the security of his valuable ring, Rabbi Yehudah lent him a considerable sum, to be returned as soon as Rabbi Shemuel repaid the loan, for the ring was a cherished family heirloom.

Rabbi Shemuel opened a small pharmacy in Malaga like the one he had operated in Cordoba. He employed Rabbi Yitzchak in his store and arranged a similar position for Rabbi Yonah ibn Janach with one of his merchant associates. As before, he was free during most of the hours of the day to pursue his Torah study, since the business did not exact more than a few hours each day. Here, however, he ceased to be the retiring person he had been and, before long, attracted many disciples with whom he shared the wealth of his knowledge in all areas of the Torah, such as Chummash, Hebrew grammar, Mishnah, and especially Gemara. In addition he taught his best students the art of poetry and meter. He himself was such a master of this art that he was able to express any idea whatsoever in poetic form almost as quickly as he could in prose. In fact his personal letters were mainly written in rhyme. His older pupils, who already had a basic groundwork in Mishnah and Talmud, were also taught the sciences of astronomy and logic.

Rabbi Yehudah ibn Gabirol's son, Shelomoh, was later to join the circle of Rabbi Shemuel's disciples. He excelled in his studies, and Rabbi Shemuel predicted a great future for him. He taught him the entire Talmud in depth and also initiated him into the art of poetry. Great indeed was his joy and the joy of the boy's parents when Shelomoh ibn Gabirol fulfilled the hopes they had placed in him; he was to become one of the great Torah scholars whose *piyyutim* (liturgical poems) are partially preserved to this day.

Throughout all this time, however, Rabbi Shemuel could not become used to the idea that his parents had found their death in the fire. He hoped and prayed that they might have been saved and that he would yet see them alive. And for this very reason he could not find consolation, for our Sages teach that "it has been decreed that the dead shall be forgotten, but not the living." He tried to banish the anguish from his heart by expressing his innermost thoughts in the form of poems, which were later edited, mainly by his sons, in three anthologies: *Ben Tehillim, Ben Mishley,* and *Ben Koheleth.* Another source of comfort and encouragement during these hard times was his constant study of the Torah and teaching it to his beloved students.

5
the royal scribe

The city of Malaga is ancient indeed: as far back as Roman times it harbored a Jewish settlement. The first Jews reached it together with the Phoenicians, founders of the city. At the time of our story, Malaga was one of the major commercial cities, and since much of its trade was concentrated in Jewish hands, many Jewish merchants visited it from all corners of the land, and even from distant Germany, in order to barter the products of their land — bear pelts, copper, shields and spears — for citrus fruit and wine.

These merchants naturally heard about Rabbi Shemuel and visited his shop in order to converse with him and ask him questions concerning the Torah. And when they returned to their birthplace, Germany, which had boasted many great Torah scholars ever since the time of the destruction of the second beith hamikdash, they would tell their brethren there of the new light that shone in Spain, the man who was wise both in Torah and in every branch of knowledge. Rabbi Shemuel in turn gained new information about the nature and customs of various nations and lands, and learned how to deal with people of dissimilar habits, a knowledge which helped him greatly later in life.

In those times few people were literate, especially among the non-Jews. Since Rabbi Shemuel knew Arabic perfectly and had mastered many other languages, people would occasionally ask him to write their business or personal letters. He would oblige for a small fee, and this provided him with an additional income, again "a clean and simple craft" which did not detract much from his study. He had to write these letters in many languages, for the city was populated by people from assorted lands and races, and the merchants who came there from all the corners of the world added to its potpourri of languages.

Once, for example, an Egyptian Jewish merchant whose business dealings required him to send uniform notifications to many different officials and merchants in other countries asked Rabbi Shemuel to write letters for him in Arabic, Aramaic, Hebrew, Latin, Castilian, and Greek. His business affairs later brought him to Babylonia, where he told Rav Hai Gaon about Rabbi Shemuel, and a steady correspondence soon developed between the two. Since postal service did not exist over such vast distances at that time, Rabbi Shemuel would send his letters to Rabbeinu Nissim in Kairwan, from where they would be relayed to Babylonia to Rav Hai Gaon, and vice versa.

Just like the newspaper and soft drink stands of our times which stand in the middle of the squares of major

[Shemuel Hanagid

cities, so were the stands set up by peddlers and public scribes at the time of our story, in the middle of the large city squares. Rabbi Shemuel's pharmacy, too, stood in such a place, the broad plaza in front of the splendid palace of Abu-el-Kassim ibn el-Arif, the vizier and scribe of the Caliph Khabus of Granada. This caliph was especially particular about the orderly management of his huge estate, which included extensive orchards and vineyards, and he required that the vizier who managed his affairs in Malaga send him a detailed written account of the state of his property to Granada. The vizier turned to Rabbi Shemuel, whose shop was near his palace, and entrusted him with the preparation of these written accounts. These reports, written in a beautiful poetic Arabic, aroused the vizier's astonishment. He was especially enthusiastic about the comments that were written in the margins of the account, for they contained sundry suggestions on how to improve the state of the property and increase the productivity of the orchards and vineyards.

One day, he ordered Rabbi Shemuel to appear before him. "Wise and learned man!" the vizier addressed him when he entered the grand palace. "It is not fitting for a man blessed with your literary talents to sit under such a puny awning. Do me the honor of joining me in my luxurious palace, and be my scribe to the end of days!"

Rabbi Shemuel did not find the courage to refuse the request of this powerful man, who was in effect the ruler of the land, since Caliph Khabus of Granada did not do anything without consulting him first. Although Rabbi Shemuel recalled the warning of our Sages, "Do not become familiar with the government," he nevertheless saw himself forced to accept the vizier's offer, and resolved to use his proximity to royalty for the benefit of his brethren.

The Jewish communities in Spain, by this time, considered Rabbi Shemuel as the leader of their generation. Rabbi Chanoch, his teacher, had died in Cordoba in a most saddening manner. On Simchath Torah, he had mounted the *bimah* (synagogue platform) as *Chathan Torah* (one who recites the blessings over the reading of the last portion of the Torah) as he did each year, accompanied by the leading members of the congregation. Suddenly the bimah collapsed under them — its boards being ancient and rotten — and Rabbi Chanoch, who was then very old, broke his collarbone and died that day.

After the expulsion from Cordoba, his disciples were dispersed to various places, where they established new yeshivoth and Torah centers; the greatest of these disciples, Rabbi Shemuel, had before long virtually become the spiritual leader of the Jewish community in Spain. Consequently his new proximity to royalty had a double significance.

6
Granada

In the course of his duties, Rabbi Shemuel was forced to leave Malaga and accompany his new employer across the mountains to Granada. His importance grew from day to day in the eyes of the vizier, who could not stop marveling at the wisdom of his new scribe. When he began conversing with him about diplomacy and politics, he revealed a rare and amazing grasp of the most complicated matters. In addition to his brilliant capabilities, Rabbi Shemuel also displayed staunch loyalty and self-sacrifice.

Caliph Khabus lived a life of revelry and, as a result, was always pressed for money. One day he needed a gigantic sum and imposed upon the vizier the task of extracting it from the ten richest people of Granada. How should this money be raised? That did not interest him. As far as he was concerned, there was no reason to stop at murder, if this should prove necessary. The vizier was in a quandary. He knew that there was no way out of this predicament. As matters stood, he was not particularly popular, and it was clear to him that the powerful men of the city would plot his death as a result of this affair. On the other hand, if he did not provide the necessary sum he would have to pay with his head. In his despondency he turned to his scribe, Rabbi Shemuel, and asked his advice.

"How much is all your property worth?" Rabbi Shemuel asked.

"All my cash assets add up to approximately the necessary figure," the vizier replied.

"In that case, listen to my advice and give the caliph all of your personal fortune rather than bring upon yourself the wrath of the powerful men of Granada. You can amass a new fortune — but you can never grow a new head!"

The vizier heeded his Jewish scribe's advice. It was not long before his deed became known throughout the city and, as a result, the attitude of the people toward him changed completely. The caliph was also deeply moved by his loyalty and rewarded him with valuable gifts, so that in the end his sacrifice was repaid many times over.

Things could not have looked more promising — until one day, suddenly, the vizier fell seriously ill and Rabbi Shemuel was once again faced with a turning point in his life.

7 kidnap and ransom

"You set darkness and it is night; in it all the animals of the forest move about." Thus the Psalmist (104:20) describes how, when all are fast asleep and the world is still in the dark of night, then comes the hour for all kinds of poisonous creatures to venture from their holes to harm man and animal. So too, when stormy revolutions change the daily pattern of life, wicked people of all descriptions creep out of their lairs to reap benefit from the state of confusion.

At the time of our story, when the first breath of a rumor circulated that the great city of Cordoba was to be destroyed, veterans of the underworld converged upon it from every side with the intent to rob, murder, and riot. Many pirates also rushed to the scene, but they were not so avid for gold and silver, or even for precious gems and pearls, as for human beings whom they could sell as slaves in distant lands for exorbitant prices. In those times the brazenness of the Norman and African pirates reached such proportions that the whole land of Spain, which is almost entirely surrounded by water and thus bore the brunt of pirate activities, was held in their thrall.

The pirates would often penetrate deep inland, leaving their ships under the watch of their dutiful wives and children, and would take up carefully camouflaged positions close to the narrow mountain passes. Terror of these brigands was so great that citizens were granted legal permission to kill any pirate who crossed their path, without trial. During the destruction of Cordoba, however, these pirates had a free hand. In fact, the new ruler was even pleased to witness the suffering of the inhabitants he hated.

Rabbi Shemuel's parents were quietly conversing inside their house near the river bank, when bandits burst in. One of them, a burly, terrifying fellow, grabbed Rabbi Yosef in his mighty hand and dragged him to one of the small boats anchored in the nearby river. For some reason the bandits left his frail wife unharmed, perhaps because they had not noticed her.

Rabbi Yosef suffered unspeakable indignities in his foul cabin, deep in the hold of the pirate vessel, as it lurched its way eastwards across the Mediterranean, past the forbidding coasts of Sardinia and Sicily. Finally, it anchored at the fortified port city of Taranto, on the "heel" of Italy, just in time for the big market day for slaves. The huge market square teemed with traffic, and the noise of the brisk business, the shouts, and the fights, was enough to deafen the ears of anyone brave enough to venture there.

A group of Negroes stood near one of the stands, bound together in one long chain. They gnashed their teeth angrily whenever a new client ventured to inspect them. In their hearts beat the hope of revenge some day. Woe unto the buyer who acquired them; some day they would yet repay by violent death all the beatings that he had in store for them. For the present, however, they must tell any prospective buyer what they were suited for, whether house or field work.

At another stand sat a disconsolate group of youths from Germany: brigands had found them on an island on the verge of starvation. People marveled at their light hair, white skin, and blue eyes. Nevertheless, it was difficult to find a buyer willing to pay a high price for them since they did not know the language of the land or any of its customs. In the end a wandering minstrel bought them cheaply in order to use them in his productions.

In one corner of the great market, far removed from Rabbi Yosef and his captors, stood a group of twelve men, some of whom wore the dignity of age, their heads bent and eyes glued to the ground. The hands of these men were not fettered for their captors felt certain that they would not escape. Silently their lips recited the verses of *Tehillim* (91:1): "He who sits in the lee of the Most High, abides in the shadow of the Almighty. I will say of Hashem: He is my refuge and my fortress, my God in Whom I trust."

These were Jews captured in their flight from Cordoba and now being offered for sale in the slave market. As soon as the local Jews had heard of the calamity that had befallen Cordoba, they knew that Jewish captives would be brought to the slave market to be sold and had therefore prepared a large sum in order to redeem them. And indeed, a man of venerable appearance approached this group of captives. Clearly he was no ordinary fellow, but one of the scholars of the city come in person to perform the mitzvah of redeeming captives. He turned to the trader and began to discuss the price.

According to halachah, a Jewish captive should not be redeemed for more than he is worth — as our Sages taught in the Mishnah of *Gittin*. In their wisdom the Sages made this a firm binding rule, so that bandits would not grow avaricious and devote their time to capturing Jews, assuming that other Jews would redeem them at any price. Indeed, it was known among slave-traders and outlaws that Jews did not redeem captured people or holy writings (such as Torah scrolls) for more than their ordinary market value. Moreover, these pirates and bandits used to treat the Jews more humanely and decently than other captives, knowing that as a rule they would not try to escape. This too was because of the halachah: for Jewish law forbids any attempt to help captives escape — so as not to put any human life in danger.

"I am very sorry," the trader said to the Jew who had come to redeem his fellows, "but I cannot sell you these men at the price you offer me. These men are veritable gems. You won't find many like them. These are scholars, intelligent and educated. Let them copy books, or teach children, and you'll easily get your money's worth."

"The price that I offered you is the highest that I can give you for them," answered the Jew decisively. "You know that according to our Law it is forbidden to pay for a captive more than he is worth, and these men are no longer young. I will not be able to have much use of them and they are not worth more than the sum I suggested."

"Very well," answered the trader, "take them. But I am only doing this for you because I've taken a liking to you and I know that if you were able to, you would give me more out of your own good will."

This trader possessed the characteristic of Efron the Hittite — he said much and did little. In the end, his client was forced to count out two full purses of gold coins.

When the sale was completed, he approached the captives, who were still standing with heads downcast, murmuring the verses of *Tehillim*: "You will not be afraid of terror by night, nor of the arrow that flies by day; nor of the pestilence that walks in darkness, nor of the destruction that wastes at noon." And he continued with them aloud: "A thousand may fall at your side and ten thousand at your right hand; it shall not approach you."

Surprised and happy, the men immediately straightened up, their eyes expressing their joy.

"*Shalom aleichem* (Peace be with you), my dear brothers!" their benefactor greeted them pleasantly. "You are free to do as you please, with the help of God. Does not the Torah thus say: For the Jews are slaves unto Me — and not slaves to slaves? I am truly happy to be privileged to fulfill the mitzvah of pidyon shevuyim."

"Peace unto you!" replied the captives thankfully. "Please be so kind as to tell us what your name is, gracious brother."

"My name is Nissim. I came here a while ago from the city of Kairwan and have had the privilege of encouraging our brothers here to redeem Jewish captives."

"Rav Nissim Gaon of Kairwan!" the captives exclaimed in amazement. "A leading figure of Jewish leaders had to exert himself for our sake?"

"And so what of it?" countered Rav Nissim. "Do you begrudge me the privilege of fulfilling such an important mitzvah? Come now to my house. The local townsfolk have already prepared food and lodging for the captives whom they expected to be freed today. Tomorrow we will consider how to establish you financially. We may be able to inquire as to the whereabouts of the members of your families in order for you to be reunited with them."

"We are most grateful to you, our great teacher," cried one of the captives, "for the kindness which you have shown in concerning yourself with this mitzvah and arousing the people of the city to perform it as well. May your good deed be rewarded by the God of Yisrael. I am a student of the beith midrash in our city, and have had the privilege of hearing Torah lectures from Rabbeinu Mosheh ben Chanoch and from his son, Rabbeinu Chanoch. I was captured en route to collect money for the yeshivah scholars. Now, having heard of such a worthy community in your city, I desire to stay with you, if it pleases you."

"Praised be the God of Yisrael," answered Rav Nissim, "that we have gained a talmid chacham for this city. The people here will surely feel happy to support a scholar and authority who is well-versed in the Talmud. If it please God, after I have gotten to know you better, I will recommend you to them. I myself am about to return to my city, Kairwan."

And with this, Rabbeinu Nissim returned to his lodgings together with the captives, filled with joy at the mitzvah that had come his way, especially since he had been able to redeem a scholar.

We can imagine his sorrow, had he known that a short distance away, at the other end of the very same market place, an honored personality was being offered for sale — the father of his beloved friend Rabbi Shemuel, Rabbi Yosef Halevi!

8
a sage in bondage

In the city of Taranto, which, at the time of our story, was being fought over by the Byzantine Emperor and the Saracens, there was always an officer of the Bhevide royal family whose job it was to visit the slave market and choose those slaves most suitable to serve in the royal court. The Bhevides, descended from an ancient Persian dynasty, were the three sons of the minister Bheva. They had captured Persia in 4594 (834 C.E.) and established an independent kingdom in it. The youngest of the brothers, Miz Ad-Dula, had captured the capital city after eleven years of battle and ruled there under the title of Emir El-Umarah. At the time of our story, the rule of the Bhevide brothers had spread over all Mesopotamia and Persia.

Another of the brothers, the emir Biha Ad-Dula, who ruled in the region of what had formerly been Babylonia, maintained his court on a high cultural level. In fact his was the most magnificent court in the Middle East, and the home of the greatest scholars and poets, including the famous Bironi and Firduzi. It was for the emir Biha that the Bhevide slave buyer wandered that day in the Taranto market place, and

[Shemuel Hanagid

haggled over the puchase of Rabbi Yosef, whom he eventually took to the land of Babylonia.

The pride of this ruler was his well-stocked library. One large and airy room in it was constantly occupied by his slaves, the scribes and bookbinders, who copied all the most ancient and rare books, and bound them in impressive luxurious bindings. Rabbi Yosef, an expert in curing fine parchment for bindings, was added to the staff of the library workers, and employed as well in transcribing books, since he knew Arabic script perfectly.

The status of these scribes and binders was much better than that of the other slaves, for in general they were learned people, respectable and refined, whose bad luck had caused them somehow to fall into the disgrace of slavery. Rabbi Yosef was fortunate to enter the society of these people, so that he did not have to suffer the trials of an undesirable environment in addition to the ills of servitude. Even from the standpoint of food the lot of the library slaves was much better than that of the others, although this fact did not affect Rabbi Yosef, who never tasted the court food, subsisting only on figs, dates, and carobs.

During peace time the emir Biha himself liked to spend long hours in his large library. Although he had been trained from youth as a warrior rather than a scholar, he nevertheless had a natural affinity for academic subjects which encouraged him to dedicate many hours to study. On occasion, he also liked to

A Sage in Bondage]

examine his new books and enjoy their attractive appearance without actually reading them. His attention was therefore soon drawn to the fine craftsmanship of Rabbi Yosef, who also had a talent for ornate calligraphy. Biha began to converse with him and immediately realized that here was an honest, intelligent man, gifted with a brilliant power of elucidation. From then on, the emir used to love to hold conversations with his new servant, to the extent that his royal pride allowed him to converse with a slave.

Five times daily, huge martial drums would pound out their calls at the palace gates. After the fifth time, three hours before sunset, all the servants of the palace were free to go out and refresh themselves wherever they pleased. Rabbi Yosef took advantage of those free hours to grow acquainted with the flora of the land and to study which medicines could be produced from the various herbs. Within a short time this became known in the court of the emir and whoever required any kind of medicine would turn to him.

One day Emir Biha suddenly became ill and took to his bed. The efforts of his doctors to reduce his high fever were unsuccessful and, left with no choice, they turned to Rabbi Yosef and asked him to try his hand. Rabbi Yosef, through his skill and dedication, succeeded in reducing the dangerous fever and within a short time the emir recovered from his sickness. From that time on a strong bond of friendship was formed between the emir and the rabbi, and they would spend

[Shemuel Hanagid

many hours together each day. The emir even included Rabbi Yosef in his entourage on long excursions — an unheard-of privilege for a slave. From day to day he learned to appreciate more and more the great wisdom and refined soul of his new acquaintance, and his respect for him grew.

9
the ruler and the rabbi

During their walks, the emir and Rabbi Yosef would sometimes reach the place called Hila on the left bank of the Euphrates River. There stood four huge mounds — the ruins of Babylon, once the most magnificent of all the cities of the world. These awesome ruins now served as a source of building materials for the construction of Seleucia and Ctesiphon on the Tigris River, and afterwards for the construction of the cities of Kufa and Baghdad.

When Rabbi Yosef first saw the ruins of Babylon, he recited the blessings that our Sages ordained, "Blessed is He Who destroyed wicked Babylon." When he saw the ruins of the palatial home of Nevuchadnetzar, the ruler who destroyed the first beith hamikdash, he proclaimed, "Blessed is He Who destroyed the home of wicked Nevuchadnetzar." At the site alleged by the people of the area to have been the lion's den into which Daniel was thrown, he said, "Blessed is He Who performed a miracle for *tzaddikim* in this place." He recited this blessing as well when he reached the place which the local residents claimed to be the site of the furnace into which Chananyah, Mishael, and Azaryah

[Shemuel Hanagid

were thrown. When he saw a large ruin of stones which had served in its day for the worship of Mercolis (Mercury), he proclaimed, "Blessed is He Who extirpated idolatry from this place. And just as You have extirpated it from this place, so shall You extirpate it from all places, and return the heart of their worshipers to serve You."

Rabbi Yosef explained the content of the blessings to Biha and added that had he seen the actual idols he would have recited the blessing, "Blessed is He Who has extended His patience to those who violate His will." But since the Muslims had destroyed all the idols and statues, he recited a different blessing.

"If that is so," smiled Biha, "then we Arabs caused a change in your prayer!"

"That's right," answered the rabbi. "So we see that our monotheism was spread by you among the gentiles. And this is a sign that Hashem is preparing the world for the coming of the Messiah through whom all will recognize the truth of our holy Torah and of the prophecy of Mosheh our teacher, of blessed memory."

As soon as Rabbi Yosef had uttered these words he regretted them. "Who knows," he thought, "how the emir will react to them?" However, after a moment's consideration, the emir said, "It may be that you are partly right — though there have remained remnants of idol worship even among us. For example, there are places where we have not yet succeeded in uprooting the custom of throwing stones, as required by the

The Ruler and the Rabbi]

worship of Mercury. The religious leaders explain to the masses that throwing the stones is intended to banish Satan, in order that they should not believe in Mercury. It is nevertheless a remnant of idol worship. Who knows, there may yet come a day when your religion will spread throughout the entire world."

One morning, their conversation turned on the variety of things that make men happy.

"Many years ago," said Biha, "I chanced to visit, in the course of a tour of my kingdom, the vicinity of Pumbaditha, the majority of whose inhabitants are Jews. I passed through a middle-sized village and saw a lively hustle and bustle throughout the large market square. People with serious faces were passing to and fro, stopping at various booths and inspecting some merchandise with special care. When one of them would finally leave the market, he walked out ceremoniously, his face shining with joy, like one who has found a cache of pearls and gems. I wondered what was the nature of that merchandise which caused such joy, but all I saw in the booths were green palm branches, myrtle and willow branches, and citrons. The royal representatives in the village explained that the Jews were about to celebrate a yearly holiday called the Feast of Tabernacles, in which they took up these four species and shook them in honor of their God, and since every person tries to procure the best and choicest of each kind, they come to buy them several days before the holiday. As they were explaining, a Jew passed in front of them, his face shining with joy and his hands bearing the four species with awe, much as a mother would hold a newborn child in her arms. I wanted to gain an insight into his train of thought and called him. Without releasing his hold on the branches and citron, he bowed before me. I asked him what his profession was and, to my great surprise, he replied that he was a farmer who barely eked out a living. Nevertheless, he had just purchased these species with the income from two weeks' work. I couldn't help expressing my surprise at this, but he answered me with a glowing face that the performance of the commandment gave him happiness and strength to live.

"Still, I couldn't understand from what source this Jew and all his friends draw their spiritual strength. I thought then that these were uneducated people but here I see that you too, an educated and intelligent person, rejoice in the fulfillment of a commandment with a similar strange joy. Perhaps you can explain to me what it is?"

"It is difficult to explain such a thing," said Rabbi Yosef. "Can you, my master the emir, explain to me why a person loves his father and mother? Why a mother loves her child? It is ingrained in the soul of a man to feel love toward his flesh and blood, and we can in no way explain the laws of nature. We can merely investigate the various phenomena of nature and observe their development, but it is impossible to fathom the secret of the prime and independent cause of the laws of nature, for this prime cause is completely the will of the Creator and beyond the limit of human comprehension. Our love for the Holy One, blessed is He, is as unfathomable as the love of a son for his father. We prefer this love above all other loves in the world, even the love of our forefathers, as was stated by the prophet Isaiah, 'For You are our Father, our Savior, Your Name is from the beginning of time.' This feeling, that God is our Father, is stamped in the heart of every Jew, not only by virtue of his education and his upbringing, but because the Almighty Himself planted it in our hearts, as the Torah states, 'You are sons to Hashem, your God.' We are truly His sons and He is truly our Father."

"Apparently, then," said Biha, "to cause your Creator pleasure is the very essence of your life."

"Indeed, it should be so," answered Rabbi Yosef, "for our Sages taught in the Mishnah, 'Do not be like servants who serve their master in order to receive a reward: rather be like servants who serve their master without the intent of gaining reward.' "

"Servants who serve their master without thought of gain?!" repeated Biha in astonishment. "I don't think that such a philosophy can be found anywhere else except in the Jewish religion."

"As for the other religions," ventured Rabbi Yosef, knowing by then that the emir would be tolerant enough to listen to his explanation, "Christianity and Islam are derived from of our sacred Torah. Your

[Shemuel Hanagid

prophet, Muhammad, culled from the Torah — but only what suited him. Moreoever, the ideas of our Torah have often been misinterpreted, either willfully or from lack of understanding, in order to create a contrast. Originally, for example, your Friday, the Islam day of rest, was merely a day of preparation for the Sabbath, and it became your main weekly holiday only for political reasons."

"And what about the Christian Sunday?"

"As for them, their ecclesiastic leaders, at a convention held in the Italian City of Nicea in 4085 (325 C.E.), decided to change their weekly day of rest and religious devotion to Sunday, in order to emphasize the difference between their religion and Judaism.

"About two hundred years ago, though, something strange occurred in the land of Khazar on the shore of the Black Sea. The king of the Khazars had a dream which prompted him to probe and seek the one true religion in the world. He invited a Jewish philosopher, a Christian priest and a Moslem imam for a discussion of their religions. Analyzing the proofs advanced by each one of those, the king came to the conclusion that the truth was to be found with the Jews, since both the Christians and the Moslems agreed that the Torah was the primary source of their religion. In the end, that king converted to Judaism together with many of his ministers and his people. And to this day there exists in Khazar a Jewish kingdom."

"That is interesting indeed!" exclaimed Biha.

"Truly it is amazing that there is an independent Jewish kingdom in these times! I have never heard of it."

The relationship between Rabbi Yosef and the emir grew closer and closer until the people of the royal court began to treat the rabbi like the wise and learned man he was rather than like a slave. And, in the course of time, Emir Biha became more and more influenced by his words, and slowly but surely abandoned his wild habits and his uncouth behavior.

10 the power of the pen

Meanwhile, two and a half thousand miles west of his enslaved father, and oblivious to his fate, Rabbi Shemuel maintained his pharmacy in Malaga. He continued to study Torah, to instruct his disciples, and to author his works. At this time he wrote out the entire *Tenach* (Torah, Prophets, and Writings) with such marvelous exactitude that his copy was later hailed as a model of precision. He also wrote ten works on grammar. Despite all this, he neglected none of his daily activities in his role of scribe to the vizier. Occasionally, he was visited by merchants and Jewish scholars from distant places and, ever seeking to expand his knowledge, he always inquired about the countries and nations of these travelers.

One day he was concentrating on his study of the Gemara so intently that he hardly noticed the door of his shop opening. Only when the door closed again with a slight bang did he raise his eyes. At the sight of the man who appeared in his doorway, a shiver swept his entire body and his face paled. That man sported on his head a jewel-studded *tarboosh* which reached his ears, wore brilliant silk Arab clothing, and in his gold belt he

The Power of the Pen]

had tucked a short scimitar studded with diamonds. It was Caliph Khabus, the mighty lord of Granada who sowed fear and terror wherever he appeared unexpectedly.

"Let my sudden appearance not cause you concern," the caliph said in a pleasant tone unusual with him, "although I have bad news for you. Your protector and employer, Abu-el-Kassim, has died."

A single glance at the caliph's face, which Rabbi Shemuel had not previously seen so close, served to define his character clearly. His low forehead seemed to indicate a low intelligence; his thin, aquiline nose expressed a tendency to anger and vengefulness; his prominent chin showed a blood-chilling sadism; yet in spite of these, a certain naiveté shone from his eyes. His full lips stamped their seal on the entire face and bore witness that lust was the most salient feature of this ruler.

"What do you intend to do now?" continued Khabus, fixing Rabbi Shemuel with a penetrating look.

The rabbi was not much affected by the possibility that he would now lose part of his livelihood. On the contrary, he hoped that he would now be able to devote more time to the study of the Torah, and to regain his former distance from royalty, as we are advised by our Sages to do. On the other hand, he realized that the caliph required a person of intelligence who would be faithful to him with all his heart and who would think and act in his stead. He imagined, therefore, that the caliph wished to maintain him in his office in the future too and accordingly answered what the caliph wished to hear so as not to antagonize him:

"My master the caliph! My path is clear to me. Until now I tried day and night to cause his excellency, the late vizier, and through him your highness the caliph, happiness and success. I think that my master the caliph has some humble office for me among the many offices of his great caliphate."

"A humble office? Surely not. Indeed, I will give you the highest office of all. You will be the grand vizier instead of Abu-el-Kassim."

These words petrified Rabbi Shemuel. Surprise and confusion crowded his mind in succession: What was he to reply to such an offer? Did not King Shelomoh warn us about this, when he requested from Hashem: "Give me neither poverty, nor wealth, lest I grow sated and deny the Name of my God"? He also called to mind the warning of our Sages, "Do not become known to the authorities, for they only befriend a person for their own benefit, pretending to be his friends but not standing by him in his time of need."

On the other hand, the Jews were persecuted from all sides, and the name Yisrael was the butt of mockery and ridicule among the nations. Torah scholars suffered want and the knowledge of Torah was continually on the wane. By holding such high office in the government he might be able to raise the banner of Torah, and to lighten the lot of his Jewish brethren . . .

The Power of the Pen]

These thoughts raced through his mind for only a brief moment; he had to give his reply to the caliph immediately and could not afford to indulge in speculation and pondering. In the end he decided to try to reject the offer, if at all possible.

"Pardon me, my master the caliph," Rabbi Shemuel said humbly. "I am a Jew, a member of that race that does not believe in the sanctity of the Koran. Surely you are aware that Muhammad, your prophet, succeeded in bringing all of the peoples of Arabia into the covenant of his faith except for the Jews, who preferred to sacrifice their lives rather than change their religion. You must understand that I am not fit to be a vizier in an Arab country."

As he said these last words, Rabbi Shemuel discerned signs of anger on the face of the caliph. "What have I done?" he thought in fear. "Who knows what misfortune I have brought upon myself because of my opposition to the tyrant's words?"

"There is no mistake here!" the caliph cried in mock severity. "And in order to show you what caused me to choose you specifically, let me tell you this: I have come now directly from the house of the vizier, whose scribe you were. I was present when he died. Before his death I expressed to him my sorrow that I was about to lose as faithful, talented and wise a servant as he was. He rallied and said to me: 'My master the caliph! Lately it was not I who advised you on my own; rather, all my advice was from my scribe,

בן משלי

תרח
יעלים עיניו ירא אל לבלתי / יו"ד / בוא בריבות כי מריבות חנוטש
... ... / / ... ... ילוטש

תרט
יעמוד מלך בראשית בשקדו / לאביר רעים ואמץ קדושים
באשר עומל בכרם נטיעה / יהי חם עלי שורק וקץ את באושים

תרי
יצא לך מים / מאש אשר תֻחְתָה
עתים וכמה קם / אבל בבית משתה

הנגיד

תריא
כף. / כף.
כבוד מלך בקהל רב ובוז / במשיב על דבר פיהו בקהל / ח
וטוב נמצא לשוכן ים ושכן / למלך באשר שָׁכַן ואהל

תריב
כראש נָשָׂא בגוף מלך ורביו[1] / כידיו וחילותיו כזֻנֻב / י
ואדמתו בכרם בעבודה / פרי יעש ושוכניה כְעָנָב

תריג
כרוכב הארי עובד מלכים / ומי זה הֹארִי יעל עלי גב / ג
ישוגב משאר חיות בשכנו / מעונתו וזמנהו לא ישוגב

תריד
כמו אחת אשר יהגו בני איש / בפה אחד בטובה אין שנִיה / י
כיד נדיב מָמַלָּא פה לשבעה / ומזלות עלי צמא רְוָיָה

תרטו
כאל עליון אשר יַחַד בחסדו / ותוכחותיו ואין ממרה כנגדו / ד
אלהים[2] הממונה על אנשים / להעמידם ולנחותם לבדו

תרטז
כמה לשון בעט סופר מליצים / שניהם בלבבך ספרו חק
לשון אדם ... ... / ... ...

---
[1] פי' ושריו.
[2] פי' שופט מן אלהים לא תקלל (שמות כ"ב כ"ז).

A page of R. Shemuel Hanagid's poetry (published from manuscript in Oxford, 1934). Above verse no. 611 appears the word Hanagid, *for it is spelled out by the letters next to last in the first lines of the verses that follow.*

The Power of the Pen]

the Jew Shemuel, to whom none can compare in intelligence in all respects. Set your eye on him and appoint him as minister and adviser, for then you are assured of success as I succeeded until now.' So you see that you have no excuse to evade the position I have offered you. Allah himself desires it, for the words of a man on his deathbed border on prophecy."

Rabbi Shemuel was left with no alternative but to obey Khabus and accept the high office. That same night the caliph sought his advice in connection with certain political affairs which had had to be postponed during the late vizier's illness, and had him compose several secret letters. The convincing style of these letters aroused Khabus's admiration.

On the following day negroes in red uniforms appeared in the streets of Granada. They trumpeted loudly and proclaimed ceremoniously that the Jew, Shemuel of Cordoba, then twenty-eight years of age, had been appointed as vizier — the advisor and scribe to the caliph.

Toward evening this event was celebrated at an official ceremony held in the caliph's court. All the celebrities and ministers of state sat at lavishly arranged tables, at which welcoming speeches were held to honor the new vizier. Though it was his first public appearance as vizier, Rabbi Shemuel bore himself like a veteran in the company of these princes and dignitaries, completely at ease, sometimes even hiding a faint smile, while he listened to the smooth

[Shemuel Hanagid

words of flattery from the members of the court who sought to find favor with him.

Returning home late that night, he expressed his feelings about this eventful day in three poems. In one magnificent hymn he thanked his Creator for this great turning point in his life, attributing his success to his trust in Him. At the same time, he admonished himself not to become too proud of his power and fame, to remain humble, and to continue to put his entire trust in Hashem:

> Whether you toil little or a great deal,
> In this world you will have your meal,
> By just a bit of work — some bread you'll have,
> So what does it help you if you slave?
> You may serve kings — but all your gains
> Will merely profit — your mortal remains.
> At peace, thou soul! Travail forfend,
> Your beginning is in God's hand — and so is your end!

In another poem he praised the pen, for it was by means of the pen — the instrument of the scribe — that he had been elevated to his high position:

> Hold a pen,
> Wield a quill,
> For with these is a fortune
> Amassed at will.
> Pens raise the lowly;
> Quills speak in script
> On the tongues of kings
> If in wisdom's ink dipped.

Another poem on the same subject:

> The brilliance of a man
> In his writing you may scan;
> And the embers of his wisdom
> His pen can quench or fan.
> A king with scepter rules;
> *Pens* are the sage's tools.

On another occasion, Rabbi Shemuel wrote of his deep love for Eretz Yisrael and the intense longing of *Keneseth Yisrael* in exile to return to "her first husband" — *Hakadosh Baruch Hu* (God). Especially at this hour, having reached the pinnacle of his personal success, Rabbi Shemuel contemplated with doubled pain the lot of the Jewish people scattered amongst strange nations — its own country deserted, and its Temple in ruins.

11 by the waters of Babylon

One of those seemingly-forgotten exiles, of course, was Rabbi Shemuel's own father, Rabbi Yosef, alone and forlorn by the waters of Babylon. His master, the emir Biha, was generous to him, it is true, but this attitude did not comfort him for the loss of his family, nor lessen his concern for their fate. But before we continue our story, we must briefly survey the political situation as it was then in Baghdad.

In these days — the days of Rav Hai Gaon — the Jews of Babylonia were subjects of the caliph of Baghdad, El Khadir, the Mighty One. The Jewish community had been deprived of its autonomy and had to submit to the jurisdiction of the caliph's chief justice, a notoriously unjust *kadi* (judge) of the fanatical Moslem Sunnite sect. The community was a prime target for his arbitrariness and he took every opportunity to fine and imprison the Jews and their leaders.

Accusations of the Jews were all too easy to come by — thanks mainly to the Karaite sect's hatred for the Geonim and the Jewish community. This dissenting Jewish sect, founded in the eighth century by Anan, made it a practice to falsely denounce the Rabbanite Jews. The kadi, of course, was pleased enough to take advantage of these accusations, gratifying his own vindictiveness and, at the same time, filling the caliph's chronically empty treasury.

During the period of the annual *yarchey kallah* months (Adar and Elul), the Jewish community was particularly vulnerable, for during that time thousands from surrounding cities and villages would assemble in the yeshivoth, setting aside their usual business and tax payments, and dedicating all of their time to the intensive study of Torah *shebe'al peh* and Torah *shebichthav* — the Oral and the Written Law, respectively. On this pretext the kadi would imprison many of them and confiscate their property. One bitter day, the greatest leader of the community, respected throughout the Jewish world — Rav Hai Gaon — was convicted by this kadi. He was thrown into prison and all his property was confiscated. The many efforts and attempts of Babylonian Jewry to free the leader of their generation were in vain. The caliph, to whom a delegation turned in complaint, refused their petition with mockery and ridicule.

Rabbi Yosef knew nothing of all these events, for he was far removed from the centers of Jewish life. The emir, who wanted to enjoy his wisdom as they discussed Greek philosophy together, made available to him his most precious manuscripts from the Syrian and Arabic translations of Aristotle's works, written on parchment scrolls. For example, he had recently brought him a celebrated commentary on Aristotle's works written by Abu-Yussuf-el-Kandi, who had lived about one hundred and fifty years before the time of our story and had won fame as a physician, mathematician, astrologer, and philosopher.

Eventually, in the course of their discussions, the emir became aware of Rabbi Yosef's depression because of his separation from his family and environment. He therefore tried to make him feel better by giving him preferential treatment. One day, however, an incident occurred which was to change the course of Rabbi Yosef's life.

On that day the emir was in high spirits. His prime enemy, Shanzim Ad-Dulla, had suddenly been murdered by insurgents and his military chief had gone over to Biha's side. As a result of this, the cities of Butzistan, Paras, Karaman and Pumbaditha had fallen into Biha's hands, and the emir's elation was apparent in his discussion with the rabbi in the great throne-hall that morning. Suddenly, the lofty portals were thrown open, and two negro slaves entered, prostating themselves before the emir. Biha motioned to them to rise and speak.

"Our master the emir! A delegation on behalf of the Jewish yeshivah of Pumbaditha requests to be given audience, in order to make an appeal against caliph El Khadir and his chief justice, the Sunnite."

Emir Biha, who only a moment before had been

discussing profound philosophical and humane ideas, suddenly reverted to his own former self:

"These Moslem-haters! Let them pay their fines and leave me alone with their complaints. I have no time to receive their delegation."

Rabbi Yosef pricked up his ears. A delegation on behalf of the yeshivah in Pumbaditha! The words of *Megillath Esther* suddenly came to his mind: ". . . who knows whether you have not come to royal estate for such a time as this?" Perhaps for this purpose Hashem had brought about his sale as a slave to the emir, so that he could serve as an advocate for his oppressed brothers? Perhaps, too, by meeting the delegation, some way would be found to free him? . . But how could he approach Biha now, while he was in such a mood, without incurring his wrath? If he failed, he would suffer a double loss: not helping the delegation, and bringing disfavor on himself. All these thoughts and many others raced through Rabbi Yosef's mind in these precious seconds. "Nevertheless," he thought, "I must not remain silent. The Torah says, 'Do not stand by while your friend's life is at stake.' " He was going to risk it.

"Forgive me, my master the emir," Rabbi Yosef ventured. "I have been fortunate to be in your presence for a long time now and to hear from your mouth words of wisdom and fairness. Far be it from you, therefore, my merciful master, to allow injustice in your kingdom. The Jews especially are worthy of your protection, more than any other nation. Apart from the believers of Islam, only the Jews believe in the true unity of God. We just discussed this point now and you, my master the emir, agreed to my words."

The expression of severity on the emir's face softened slightly.

"My merciful master," continued Rabbi Yosef, "who are the oppressors of the Jews? Are they not the Sunnites? They deny that man was given free choice between good and evil. They believe in predestination, whether for good or wicked deeds, and that man has no power to alter the decree of the Creator. If this is true, how can a Sunnite judge mete out punishment? Does he not claim that a person cannot be held responsible for his own deeds? But you, my master the emir, you belong to the sect of the Shiites, and you believe, like the Jews, that in the hand of each man rests the choice between good and evil — and it is therefore incumbent upon you to remove the Jews from the jurisdiction of their opponents and of yours, and to place them under their own and your jurisdiction. Furthermore, let us not forget the fact that the Jews are related to you, for they are descended from Noach's oldest son, like your brothers the Yishmaelites, while the Sunnites come from distant hills and from an unknown ancestry. Save your relatives from strange hands!"

"So be it," said the emir after a minute of thought. "Let the delegation enter."

The heavy crimson curtains were drawn aside to

admit seven distinguished men of venerable appearance. These were the seven *reishey kallah*, heads of the yarchey kallah, the greatest of the Babylonian Torah sages, who occupied the first rank in the beth midrash. We can imagine the overwhelming emotion Rabbi Yosef felt at beholding his first Jewish brothers in years, and world-renowned talmidey chachamim at that.

His words — and the venerable appearance of the delegation — had recalled the emir Biha into the role of the magnanimous ruler he aspired to be, and he addressed the reishey kallah respectfully:

"Are you the heads of the Jewish yeshivah of Pumbaditha?"

The sages bowed deeply.

"What a strange folk are you Jews. You have academies in Sura and Pumbaditha but you lack elementary schools like other nations. One must study the fundamentals before reaching a higher academy, is that not so?"

"Your Highness, the gracious emir, will pardon me," answered the oldest of the group of sages. "Actually, we Jews are not much in need of schools. Our children are not like children of other nations. Before they leave their parents' home their knowledge already surpasses that of those who have attended school for many years. Every Jewish home is like a school. It is an important commandment incumbent upon every Jew to teach his sons Torah. We are commanded to discuss it while we are in our homes, when we are on the road, when we go to sleep and when we arise. Nevertheless, we have maintained schools for over a thousand years. Rabbi Shimon ben Shetach was the founder of the first school system for our nation. The high priest Yehoshua ben Gamla also founded many schools."

"Who teaches in your academy?" asked the emir.

"The head of our school, or *methivta,* is called the rosh yeshivah. The teachers, of whom there are seventy, are called *allufim*. We seven, called reishey kallah, repeat the lecture of the rosh yeshivah in public, one of us on each day of the week. In addition, we deal with legal queries which reach us from all over the world and try to supply the halachic answers after discussing them with the members of the methivta."

"On whose authority," asked the emir, "is the response issued?"

"If it please Your Highness," resumed the sage, encouraged by the potentate's unexpected interest, "after the members of the methivta decide on a response to the question, it is transcribed by a secretary and finally signed and sealed by the rosh yeshivah. On the fourth Shabbath of yarchey kallah, there is a general examination of all the members of the yeshivah. The examiner is, of course, the rosh yeshivah himself. He knows how to ask questions in such a manner as to ascertain clearly the extent of everyone's progress."

"Do the answers of all the examinees always satisfy him?" asked the emir.

"Not always. Sometimes the examinee fails to answer some of the questions. Then he receives a just punishment. The rosh yeshivah rebukes him publicly, decreases his stipend, and then delineates exactly the laws that he is required to review. In the end he informs him that if the occurrence is repeated, his stipend will be canceled entirely."

"You seem to conduct your institution very strictly."

"Such strictness is very effective, and our students try diligently to succeed in their examinations."

"I would like very much once to visit your yeshivah and to be present at one of your lectures," Biha said with a smile. "However, I fear that I might also be subjected to such an exacting test."

"Your fear is unfounded, my master the emir, for besides the yeshivah students who are scheduled to be examined, there are many people of varied ages who listen to the lectures and discussions in the yeshivah court. These are called *beney tarbitza*. They are not tied down to the yeshivah schedule and are permitted to come and go as they please. I am informing your highness of this only in case you decide to visit us incognito, by surprise, for otherwise we would certainly prepare a special place of honor for you."

"Thank you," said the emir, "for having explained how your institution runs, but I am interested in

[Shemuel Hanagid

knowing what position it holds in terms of world Jewry. Here beside me sits Yussuf, a Jew from Spain, and he too feels himself bound to your academy. You Jews, wherever you are, seem to feel a bond to the yeshivoth in Babylonia. Could you, Yussuf, explain this strange phenomenon to me?"

"You should know, my master the emir," said Rabbi Yosef, "that when Moses our teacher received the Torah from Sinai, he also received from God the explanations which are recorded in the Oral Law. The main clauses of the Law are written in the Mishnah, which was compiled by Rabbi Yehudah Hanassi. The Mishnah itself has a commentary, the Talmud, of which we have two versions, one written in the Land of Israel, and the other in Babylonia. The former, which is also called *Talmud Yerushalmi*, is written in brief. Our Sages did not have the opportunity to develop it to its necessary length because of the persecutions they suffered at the hands of the Christians, who destroyed their houses of study. For the same reason, the versions of that Talmud are not sufficiently free from errors in transcription and it is difficult to obtain a perfect copy. This is not the case with the *Talmud Bavli*, the Babylonian Talmud, in which were detailed the arguments that led to the halachic decisions of the Sages of Babylonia, as they were clarified over a period of years and whose final completion lasted about another 150 years. After the compilers of the Talmud, Ravina and Rav Ashi, came the sages who explained

By the Waters of Babylon]

the Talmud, called *rabbanan sevora'ey*, and after them the geonim, the heads of the academies, whose reishey kallah are standing before you now. Thanks to these geonim the Talmud has become widespread throughout the Jewish exile, and the name of your country, Babylonia, has become famous amongst Jews wherever they are. Jewish communities from all over the world submit their questions to these geonim and, through their responsa, the wisdom of the Talmud is disseminated as far as Spain, Belgium, and even Germany. From this you can easily understand the great significance of the Babylonian yeshivoth for world Jewry."

The emir had listened intently to the words of Rabbi Yosef, and he now proceeded to hear the complaint of the delegation regarding the unwarranted imprisonment of Rav Hai Gaon. After convincing himself that the verdict had indeed been unfair, he now said: "Today I will issue a decree to the Sunnite chief justice, to immediately free your gaon and to pay him the sum of ten thousand dinars as indemnity. You must know, however, that you owe your success to this man, Yussuf, whose equal in wisdom I doubt exists upon the earth."

When the reishey kallah discovered that "Yussuf" was none other than Rabbi Yosef, the father of Rabbi Shemuel of Granada — well known to them for the scholarly questions he had sent to Rav Hai Gaon through Rabbeinu Nissim of Kairwan — they were very surprised and greatly distressed that this sage was being held in captivity. Clearly, however, this was not the time to discuss buying his freedom. They did, however, explain his importance in the eyes of world Jewry, hoping that this might influence the emir to free him from slavery. Finally, after many expressions of gratitude, they took leave of the emir and of Rabbi Yosef, the two Negro slaves drew apart the heavy crimson curtains, and the seven sages departed.

12
the peerless vizier

At the time of our story, the Iberian Peninsula — Spain and Portugal of today — was the scene of political strife and friction. The Berbers (a group of North African tribes from the Barbary Coast) ruled in Malaga and its surroundings but laid claim to the entire part of the peninsula that was inhabited by Arabs. Caliph Khabus of Granada, who had recently appointed Rabbi Shemuel as his vizier, was subservient to them. Khabus had just entered an alliance with the sole Slavic prince in Spain, Zumeir of Elmira, and together they had succeeded in repelling an attack by the kadi of Seville.

Khabus was a commoner who had risen to greatness. He was, therefore, always intent on proving that he was not a half-Barbaric ignoramus (which in fact he was), but well-versed in literature and science (which in fact he was not). In order to give the impression of nobility, he even argued that the natives of his country of origin, Kindhadsha, were not of Barbaric but of pure Arab extraction. In fact, however, his Berbers might excel in capturing fortresses, in deeds of plunder and murder — but not one of them was capable of producing a written line in faultless Arabic. As for his subjects, the Arabs, they suffered his yoke in fury and hatred. None of them could be trusted enough to serve as a reliable vizier. Khabus, therefore, desperately needed a learned and wise vizier who would not suffer by comparison with his neighbors' ministers.

Rabbi Shemuel, whose expert knowledge of Arabic was acknowledged even by Arab savants, and who was well versed in the sciences and even in politics, was truly a valuable find for Khabus. In spite of the fact that he was a Jew — he had even had the audacity to write a book arguing against Islam in general and the Koran in particular — Rabbi Shemuel was respected by the Arabs. Despite their prejudice and intolerance of Jews, they were forced to admit his expertise in mathematics, astronomy, and philosophy. There was hardly a single Arab scholar who could compete with his extensive knowledge. He had perfect command of seven languages. Moreover, he was very generous and, for the sake of peaceful relations, let even gentile scholars benefit from his wealth.

The following words of praise about him were written by the Arabic poet, Munfatlal: "You unite within you the good characteristics which others are fortunate to possess in part only. You released magnanimity from its bondage. You are as superior to philanthropists of eastern and western lands, as gold is superior to copper. Would that human creatures knew to differentiate between truth and lies, for then they would kiss your fingers alone. Rather than finding favor in the eyes of Allah by kissing the Black Stone in Mecca, they would kiss your hands, for they are the very source of happiness and mercy. Through your generosity, I was able to fulfill my heart's desire in this world, and I am hopeful that in the world to come my aspirations will also be realized in your merit. When I am in your presence, I subscribe openly to the religion that commands the keeping of the Shabbath, while when I am among my people, I attest to it secretly."

Rabbi Shemuel's closeness to royalty thus enabled him and his people to reap the benefits that went along with it. His munificence reached even distant lands, including the yeshivoth of Babylonia and Eretz Yisrael. He established a large library which contained many valuable volumes. He was particular about supplying scholars with exact, error-free copies of the Talmud and spent large sums for expert proofreaders who examined the manuscripts and winnowed out all errors due to faulty copying.

In one area alone were the Arabs unable to properly evaluate him: in his greatness in Torah. Only his fellow-Jews could fully appreciate his versatility: how was it possible for a single individual to be a disseminator of Torah to students; a statesman; the author of books on the Tenach, Hebrew grammar, and halachah; and a divinely gifted poet — at one and the same time!

13
an assassin strikes

In addition to his position as vizier, Rabbi Shemuel was appointed by the caliph to supervise customs and to prevent smuggling. He now began to feel the negative aspects of his high office, since circumstances sometimes forced him to favor one person over another or to impose punishment and fines. As a result, he acquired a number of enemies, amongst them even Jews.

The mountain ranges that constituted the border between the caliphates were especially favorable to smuggling. One band of smugglers in particular was well organized to elude the border patrol and to slip between its fingers. This band apparently had highly placed connections which they bribed generously in exchange for free access to the border, and these people grew rich at the caliph's expense.

Faithful to his obligation, Rabbi Shemuel dealt stringently with the smugglers and did not hesitate to prosecute them, even though, in the end, the traces led to the mightiest of all the royal officers — Muhammad ibn Ibrahim, a nephew of the caliph's favorite wife. Eventually, Rabbi Shemuel drew the caliph's attention

An Assassin Strikes

to Muhammad's vast wealth which could not possibly have been acquired in honest ways. The caliph, however, was not convinced by this, and demanded clearer evidence.

Muhammad owned vast tracts of land throughout the country, and smugglers used these as hideouts for themselves as well as for their loot. One day Rabbi Shmuel was informed by his agents that a consignment of merchandise worth a fortune was scheduled to arrive at a certain estate belonging to Muhammad. Rabbi Shemuel immediately sent a squad of secret police, accompanied by armed horsemen, to set an ambush. The project was successful and some ten smugglers were seized, including Muhammad himself. All of the smugglers were sentenced to death and executed — except for Muhammad. Thanks to his connections, his sentence was commuted to life imprisonment.

Now Rabbi Shemuel had made a powerful enemy, and he was well aware of this. He greatly feared the vengeance of Muhammad ibn Ibrahim's clan. True, their desire for revenge was aimed mainly at the caliph, but by eliminating Khabus they would cause their own downfall. Rabbi Shemuel, the Jewish vizier, however, was a ready victim for their violence.

As every minute of his time counted, his daily schedule followed an exact pattern. Every Shabbath, at a specific hour, he would visit his father-in-law, Rabbi Reuven, a wealthy and respected Torah scholar. At that time, all of Rabbi Reuven's sons, daughters, and other relatives would gather in his home. From there, Rabbi Shemuel would continue on to the beith midrash to lecture to his students.

His enemies, plotting against his life, realized that in his home they would have no opportunity to carry out their scheme, because of the faithful servants who always surrounded him. They therefore decided to take advantage of this weekly visit to his father-in-law and to attack him there. To eliminate any clues, they hired professional murderers from outside the city, and even prepared wagons for a quick getaway.

Their diabolic plan succeeded — almost. At the hour Rabbi Shemuel usually visited his father-in-law, two masked men with daggers drawn made their way into Rabbi Reuven's house. Rabbi Shemuel, however, had left already. Not finding their intended victim, the killers vented their wrath on whoever happened to be there, and thus murdered Rabbi Reuven and his daughter — Rabbi Shemuel's wife — as well as his sister's son, a young scholar for whom a great future had been predicted. The murderers hurried to escape after the massacre but, in his haste, one of them fell and broke his leg. He was soon seized by the neighbors who, drawn by the cries, had rushed to the site.

Through the arrest of the murderer, the cause of the crime was soon discovered. Under interrogation, he soon admitted everything; the revenge that had been planned by the powerful family of Muhammad ibn Ibrahim against Rabbi Shemuel came to light.

An Assassin Strikes

This event shocked Rabbi Shemuel to the depths of his soul. Instead of helping his brethren, as he had hoped, he had heaped tragedy upon the members of his family and had endangered all the Jews. He decided to resign from his high position, but the caliph refused to accept his resignation. He claimed that this would indicate a lack of loyalty on Rabbi Shemuel's part, who seemed thereby to prefer the pursuit of his personal affairs over the welfare of the state. This put Rabbi Shemuel in a dilemma for, while he was loath to remain in his dangerous position, he could not allow himself and his Jewish brethren to be accused of disloyalty to their country. In the end, against his will, he finally agreed to remain in the caliph's service. But he did succeed in having responsibility for the border patrol transferred to other hands. He argued that this dangerous job should not be imposed on a Jew, beset by enemies, whose life not even the government could protect, as had been sadly proven. Instead of this, however, another task was assigned to him, one not less dangerous — that of commander-in-chief of the army.

14 a tongue for a tongue

Caliph Khabus continued to appreciate Rabbi Shemuel's intelligence and energy, and took no step in matters of state, minor or major, without first consulting him.

At the moment, what concerned him most was the renovation of the Red Fortress, commonly known as El Hamra (Alhambra), the most magnificent testimony to Arab architecture in Europe. The original buildings, erected some 150 years prior to the time of our story, with their surrounding gardens and orchards, had been badly damaged by the civil war; all that remained of their former splendor was an abandoned ruin. Khabus desired it to become a most splendid structure, which would arouse the envy of the neighboring emirs. In particular, he meant it to be ready for the coming visit of his ally, Zumeir of Elmira, due to take place the following spring. This made it necessary for Rabbi Shemuel to appear before the caliph every evening, in order to discuss the progress of repairs and to decide which of the blueprints were best suited to his plan.

Rabbi Shemuel remembered the grand buildings of Cordoba before its destruction, and was able to design

A Tongue for a Tongue]

El Hamra, known also as Alhambra, a work of magnificent architecture which attracts tourists in Spain to this day.

architectural structures of breathtaking beauty. He amazed the caliph with his imaginative suggestions, which were submitted to the architects to be fully developed. It was decided to build huge halls on a gallery of carved pillars, surrounded by carefully groomed gardens, ponds stocked with goldfish, and magnificent water fountains. The pillars would be constructed of the most expensive multicolored wood, to be imported from Africa.

The contract for the supply of this timber was granted to two merchants, one Arab and the other Berber, who both lived near the palace of the caliph.

One day the Arab merchant, Abdul Malik by name, his face fixed in an obsequious expression, approached Rabbi Shemuel and begged him to give him the sole contract for procuring the wood. "The Berbers despise us," he said. "Why should a Berber be a partner in this venture? I will give you a generous share of the profits and a valuable gift as a token of my appreciation if you grant my wish."

Immediately, the words of Yosef Hatzaddik (in *Bereishith* 39:8) flashed into Rabbi Shemuel's mind: "Behold, my master does not know what goes on in his house, and all that is his he has entrusted to me . . . How can I do this great evil and sin to God?" He made it clear to Abdul Malik, diplomatically but nonethless firmly, that he would do no such thing as to grant him the sole franchise.

Abdul Malik could hardly contain his anger. Biting

A Tongue for a Tongue]

his lips, he muttered between his teeth: "You will yet see, Jew, that this will cost you dearly!"

The work of repair and renovation proceeded at a satisfactory pace. Daily Rabbi Shemuel found new ways to add grandeur and splendor to the building. Following his instructions, the workers diverted the Sierra Nevada stream, swollen with melted snow, into many small rivulets and waterfalls to course through the gardens and wings of the palace, serving as a source of water for the many ponds and fountains, and irrigating the rich vegetation of the gardens. Within the walls of the El Hamra fortress, a deep water cistern was dug to provide the inhabitants of Granada with the clearest drinking water.

Every day the caliph, accompanied by his vizier, would survey the progress of the work. At the end of his tour they would both sit at the Gate of Justice, known as Bab el Mishle, as the Arabs literally fulfilled the verse in the Bible, "Judges and police shall you set up at your gates." Every citizen could present his case, complaint, or claim and was assured of a speedy decision, which was usually also executed on the spot.

One day, they were sitting at the gate, upon whose lintel was engraved a hand, to symbolize the Biblical verse, "The hand of the witnesses will be first to kill him and the hand of the entire people last," when the Arab, Abdul Malik, approached. When permission was granted him to speak, he addressed the caliph with the following words: "Most high caliph, may the blessings

[Shemuel Hanagid

of Allah be upon you. The words which I am about to tell you now are said not only in my name but in the name of all believing Arabs, who feel it an abomination that the closest advisors to our ruler are Jews! It is most shameful for the Arab nation that members of the Jewish people stand at its head and rule it. More than all is your vizier, Shemuel, like a thorn in the eyes of all. He is a wicked, devious person, who enriches his pocket at the expense of our country. If you maintain him in his present position much longer, our country will end in destruction and ruin."

Taken aback by this allegation, the caliph shot a sharp glance at Rabbi Shemuel, who, however, in a few words, told the caliph the truth as it was: that this Arab had sought to overreach himself by taking away the business franchise from his Berber competitor, and that he, Rabbi Shemuel, had not agreed. This was why Abdul Malik was speaking against him.

Fortunately for Rabbi Shemuel, Khabus was highly insulted himself, for the Arab's attempt had, as it were, slighted his own Berber origins. He immediately pronounced him guilty of effrontery to the caliph and his vizier and, as punishment, his evil tongue to be cut off!

Abdul Malik was immediately seized and fettered and thrown into a dungeon and, according to custom, it was up to Rabbi Shemuel to carry out the sentence.

When the court session was over, Rabbi Shemuel went to the dungeon where he was imprisoned. The

Arab fell to his feet and in a heart-rending cry begged for clemency. "Rise to your feet," Rabbi Shemuel said to him, "and tell me: how much did you stand to gain in the business venture?"

"I would have gained about one thousand gold coins," replied the Arab.

"You may return home, and I will instruct my treasurers to pay you one thousand gold coins, but from now on you must keep your tongue from deceit, for 'life and death are in the hands of the tongue.' "

A week later, when the caliph and Rabbi Shemuel were again seated at the Gate of Justice, the same Arab appeared again, to the caliph's great amazement. At the caliph's exclamation of surprise, Abdul Malik replied: "My master, the caliph, I have come to confess my error to you. I have sinned, and am guilty: your vizier, Rabbi Shemuel, is the best, the noblest man on earth. May all of my curses turn into blessings, and may the blessings of our patriarch Ibrahim rest upon his head!"

"But . . . why didn't you fulfill my command?" the caliph asked Rabbi Shemuel, angry at disobedience to any of his orders.

"I did indeed fulfill your command," replied Rabbi Shemuel. "You ordered me to remove his evil tongue. Don't you hear with your own ears now, that I removed his evil tongue and replaced it with a good one?"

The caliph laughed in spite of his anger, and once again thanked Allah for having sent him such a vizier.

15 from bondage to freedom

Emir Biha, Rabbi Yosef's master, had finally come to the decision to grant his aging Jewish slave his freedom. First of all, he decided to ascertain whether the members of his family were still alive. Rav Hai Gaon, who had just been released from prison thanks to the brave efforts of Rabbi Yosef, was a most suitable mediator for this purpose.

Rav Hai had corresponded with Rabbi Shemuel when the latter was still in Malaga. Since then, however, he had not received any information concerning Rabbi Shemuel's circumstances. He therefore contacted Rav Nissim Gaon of Kairwan, who had maintained regular correspondence with Rabbi Shemuel, asking him to serve as the link between them.

On receiving the emir's letter, Rav Hai immediately sent two special emissaries. One went to the emir to inform him that Rabbi Yosef's son was well known to him, and to the best of his knowledge, he was at present serving the caliph of Granada. The second emissary went to Rav Nissim, to suggest that he accompany the elderly Rabbi Yosef on his tiring journey and, at the same time, take up his own seat in Spain.

From Bondage to Freedom]

In addition to the emir's purpose, Rav Hai had his own considerations in contacting Rabbi Shemuel through the intermediacy of Rav Nissim. The latter had become impoverished, for he had expended most of his fortune in redeeming prisoners. In Spain he would be able to find an easier livelihood, while the Jewish community in Spain would benefit from his scholarly *hashkafah*, his philosophy of life.

It was not long before Rav Nissim replied to Rav Hai, saying that he was prepared to help Rabbi Yosef but that he himself was not yet ready to move to Spain since he considered it his obligation to remain with his own disciples in Kairwan for the time being.

When the emir received Rav Hai's letter, he decided to put Rabbi Yosef to a test. He had him called in, and said to him: "After extensive inquiries and investigations, I have finally succeeded in discovering the whereabouts of your son, Shemuel. He is presently employed as a rock quarrier in the Granada mountains, and earns his daily bread with difficulty."

Rabbi Yosef's eyes lit up at the news that his son was alive. He rose from his seat, and pronounced the blessing *"shehecheyanu, vekiyemanu, vehigiyanu lazeman hazeh,"* explaining to the emir that this was a thanksgiving to God for having kept him in life, sustained him, and enabled him to reach this time at which the good news was communicated to him. He added: "As for the fact that he earns his daily bread by physical labor, this does not upset me. Many of our

[Shemuel Hanagid

sages used to support themselves by the labor of their hands. I am confident that he leads a life of righteousness — that is what makes for our happiness in this world, and for our wealth in the world-to-come."

The emir smiled and said: "I didn't quite tell you the truth, Yussuf, when I said that your son worked in a quarry. The truth is that he has risen to the highest office a Jew can possibly hold: he is the grand vizier in the court of Khabus, the mighty caliph of Granada, where science and art flourish. He is, in effect, the ruler of the land." Extending Rav Hai's letter to Rabbi Yosef, the emir continued: "Read this letter of the rosh yeshivah. Read it and rejoice!"

Trembling, Rabbi Yosef took the letter and read it, but instead of the expressions of joy the emir had expected to hear from the aged father, Rabbi Yosef heaved a sigh, and said: "True, with the help of heaven my son has attained fame — but heaven alone knows what physical and spiritual dangers lie in wait for him there. But it is enough that my son Shemuel is still alive. Would that I might see him before I die!"

The emir of course chose this moment to tell Rabbi Yosef of his decision to grant him freedom, and he immediately arranged ship passage for him.

Having been informed of Rabbi Yosef's liberation and impending journey to Spain, Rav Hai Gaon sent Rabbi Yosef a message for his son Shemuel, asking him to extend his generous support to Rav Nissim Gaon, as befitted such a great and saintly personality.

16
a suitable match

Every morning Caliph Khabus would ride his white horse beyond the outskirts of Granada, while the rays of dawn still trembled in the east. For security's sake, he did have some bodyguards at a distance, but had no companion at his side.

One day he decided to go farther than usual and enjoy the view of his villages which were built on the mountainside. He galloped up hills and down valleys. Suddenly, at a whim, he dug his spurs into the flanks of his horse. Surprised, the horse reared and broke into a dizzying gallop, throwing his rider off in one powerful sweep. To his luck, Khabus fell right into the arms of a passerby and was thus saved from landing on a craggy rock.

For a few moments he was dazed, but gradually he came to. He addressed the man who had rescued him, saying: "You have saved my life — tell me, what is your name? I would like to reward you."

"My name is Yosef ibn Migash," replied the man. "I am a Jew from Granada, and the opportunity of having saved the noble life of our most gracious caliph is my finest reward."

This Rabbi Yosef was the grandfather of the famous *rishon* (early medieval Talmudic authority) Rabbi Yosef ibn Migash (HaR"Y Migash), the disciple of Rabbeinu Yitzchak Alfasi (Rif).

Our Rabbi Yosef, then — the one who had just cushioned the caliph's tumble — was the rosh yeshivah of Granada, and also served as one of the dayyanim (judges) of the beith din of the Jewish community, together with Rabbi Yitzchak de Leon and Rabbi Nechemiah Ashkapa.

Looking at Rabbi Yosef ibn Migash, the caliph thought that he looked familiar to him. Now he remembered: at formal receptions at which officials, and among them Jewish notables, had participated, Rabbi Yosef ibn Migash had been introduced to him.

For reasons of his own, the caliph wanted to pay his debt of gratitude to Rabbi Yosef as soon as possible. He addressed Rabbi Yosef amicably: "I recall that you have a daughter of marriagable age. Is it not so?"

Hearing these words from the mouth of an unscrupulous despot, Rabbi Yosef's face filled with fear, his entire body trembled . . . he was unable to answer.

"You have nothing to fear," the caliph said. "I have only your good at heart. I thought you might consider it an honor to marry your daughter to Rabbi Shemuel, my vizier. Surely you know that his wife was murdered at the time his father-in-law's house was attacked by outlaws."

A Suitable Match

Rabbi Yosef ibn Migash hesitated a moment and said: "My master the caliph, this would be a great honor for me indeed. But I am afraid that it is not fitting for such a great personality to marry the daughter of a simple man like me."

"A simple man?" the caliph retorted. "Aren't you the head of the yeshivah and a judge of the Jewish community in Granada?"

"True, Rabbi Shemuel appointed me as head of the yeshivah, but the truth is that I am but a simple man of negligible worth. How can I put our esteemed rabbi, your vizier, in such an uncomfortable position, for it will surely not be easy for him to refuse Your Highness' request."

Khabus found it perplexing that Jewish scholars belittled their own worth, while each one highly respected his fellow. The scholars of his own nation always tried to outdo their colleagues, and woe to whoever dared treat them lightly. "Apparently," he thought, "the Torah of the Jews is not only a code of academic knowledge, but also incorporates basic moral tenets so strong and solid that good qualities, like modesty, become like second nature to those who learn it."

But now the caliph's bodyguard could be seen approaching from behind the mountain range. Their master's prolonged absence had given them concern. The caliph quickly mounted his horse, which had calmed down meanwhile, and said to Rabbi Yosef: "I

[Shemuel Hanagid

will try to repay your kind deed, but be sure not to tell anyone what has happened. Leave this place before my men arrive."

And Khabus, who was really grateful to his Jewish savior, rode directly to the house of his vizier.

From the outside, Rabbi Shemuel's house seemed simple, for he did not want to arouse the jealousy of the gentiles, but from within it was an architectural gem. The rooms were spacious, and the windows were constructed in such a way that the light coming through them enhanced the beauty of the tasteful furnishings within.

As he entered, the caliph contemplated all this with satisfaction. Rabbi Shemuel's room was pleasantly lighted, and he was seated at his table, composing a poem on a parchment scroll. When the caliph appeared, Rabbi Shemuel rose and welcomed him.

"What are you writing on that parchment?" asked the caliph.

"It is a poem," came the quiet reply, "about the life of man and his different ages."

"Please translate it for me."

Rabbi Shemuel began to read the poem to the caliph. When he had finished, the caliph cried out in amazement, "But how is it possible for a man like you to find time to dabble in poetry? Aren't you busy all the time with political and communal matters?"

"My master the caliph! We Jews, though we do appreciate worldly comforts, do not neglect our spiritual life; in fact we prefer to be occupied with the latter."

"If so," said Khabus, "why don't you forsake all matters of the world, and occupy yourself only with matters of the soul?"

"When I am placed in a position in which I must deal with worldly matters, and I perform them with the intent of fulfilling the will of the Creator, then in fact I am perfecting my soul. We call this: doing something *lesheim shamayim*, 'for the sake of heaven.'"

"But what of food?" asked the caliph.

"Even eating and drinking — if they are done with the proper intent, to preserve one's health so as to be able to serve the Creator — are included in this idea. One of the most famous Sages of the Mishnah, Hillel the Elder, as he left the beith midrash after having studied with his disciples, was once asked: 'Where is our rabbi going?' He replied: 'I am going to do a charitable deed.' When they saw that this repeated itself day after day, they asked him again: 'Is it possible that every day you have a special call to do charity?' He answered them, 'I go to bathe, thereby being charitable toward my body.'

"On another occasion, Hillel answered a similar question of a disciple by saying that he was going to perform a charitable deed to a guest in his home. He meant that he was going to eat, to sustain his soul, which is a guest in his body. Hillel intended thereby to teach his students in a tangible way that the needs of

[Shemuel Hanagid

the body, such as washing and eating, can be — and should be — performed for the sake of heaven."

Khabus was hearing new ideas. He did not hide his amazement at these thoughts, and said: "I envy you Jews! You live a life of true nobility, almost like angels. We have no concepts such as those. To us a man has a choice of only two things, either to live a life of pleasure or to suffer self-imposed tortures in order to sanctify himself. As for myself, I was never able to accept the idea that the Creator created the body only in order to subdue and punish it, to live a life of asceticism and self-abnegation as the Christians would have it. But this idea, to live a normal physical life, and yet, thereby, to fulfill the will of God, I have never heard before."

Changing the subject, the caliph now commented on Rabbi Shemuel's writing, and said: "I see that you are writing down your ideas so that they may benefit future generations. Tell me then, wouldn't it be a pity for a man like you to leave the world without issue? You didn't have children in your first marriage. Won't you consider marrying another woman?"

"It is not easy for me to find a suitable partner," replied Rabbi Shemuel.

"I have already chosen the suitable partner for you."

Rabbi Shemuel paled. He knew that the caliph was always thinking of how to influence him to marry a Moslem woman, seeing deep political significance in the possibility of his vizier becoming the son-in-law of a noble Arab family, thus removing the hatred of his anti-Jewish opponents.

"You know, my master the caliph," he replied in a voice that trembled slightly, "that I would not transgress the commandment of my God Who forbade us to intermarry with other nations."

"I intended no such thing," said the caliph. "The mate I have chosen for you is the daughter of the rosh yeshivah, Rabbi Yosef ibn Migash."

Rabbi Shemuel breathed in relief. Still, he ventured another objection, and said: "Pardon me, my master the caliph. Although such a marriage would cause me great happiness and honor, I would not dare to presume to take the daughter of the rosh yeshivah, who, in Torah learning, is infinitely greater than I am. Rabbi Yosef surely desires to marry his daughter to a great sage and not to a simple person like myself."

"You Jews!" laughed the caliph. "You are truly a strange people. On the contrary, I see that there is no match more suitable than this one. When I mentioned this proposal to Rabbi Yosef, he argued that he was too simple a man to be worthy of having you for a son-in-law. Now you claim to be too simple a man to have a father-in-law like Rabbi Yosef. If you are both such simple men, then there is no match more suitable than this one!"

Rabbi Shemuel offered no more objections.

[*Shemuel Hanagid*

An example from the Middle Ages of an illuminated, decorated kethubah—*the document of marriage that the groom gives the bride at their wedding.*

17
an unexpected wedding guest

For political reasons, the caliph insisted that his grand vizier's wedding be celebrated with pomp and circumstance in the El Hamra palace. He invited a great number of officials and emirs from neighboring countries, to show them all the splendor and majesty of the royal court and the beauty of the palace, which had recently been renovated. The Jewish community of Granada also wished to express their esteem of Rabbi Shemuel on this occasion, and crown him with the title "Chacham of the City."

Rabbi Shemuel for his part hoped to again find happiness in his marriage to the daughter of Rabbi Yosef ibn Migash. A bitter drop in his cup of happiness was the absence of his father and mother. Had he known for certain that they had died, then he would have mourned them properly and eventually been consoled, but the thought that they might still be alive, and perhaps suffering as slaves, allowed him no peace and marred his happiness.

On the morning of the day on which the wedding was to take place in the royal court, a messenger arrived for Rabbi Shemuel with a letter from Rav

[Shemuel Hanagid

Nissim Gaon of Kairwan. Rabbi Shemuel was not surprised, for he had received letters regarding halachic questions from Rav Nissim in the past. For a moment he thought to postpone reading the letter until after the celebration, but then decided to open it right away. Fortunately, he was able to concentrate on complicated matters even at a time of great emotional turmoil.

At the outset of his letter, Rav Nissim informed him of his own good health, of his success with his disciples, and of general news in the Jewish community of Kairwan. About his own financial straits, he did not mention a word. As Rabbi Shemuel read on, his eyes opened wide and his heart started pounding. He read, retraced the words, and read them a third time to make sure that his eyes had not deceived him. Rav Nissim was writing that his father, Rabbi Yosef, was still alive, that he had recently been freed from slavery, and that he was on his way to Spain . . .

"Ah, dear Almighty God!" exclaimed Rabbi Shemuel. "Thank you for allowing me to see my beloved father again. Now I can genuinely rejoice at my wedding."

After that Rabbi Shemuel rode in state to the palace of El Hamra. The festivities opened with organized games in the spacious courtyard, whose ornately sculptured fountains gushed forth perfumed water. A public chess-tournament was held, and the winners received gem-studded gold chess pieces. Seated upon an elevated, splendid throne near the guest of honor,

An Unexpected Wedding Guest]

Caliph Khabus' face shone with satisfaction. He hoped to improve the welfare of the state by means of this celebration, and nodded pleasantly to the guests.

When Rabbi Shemuel's father arrived in Granada, in order not to make too sudden an appearance, he had Rav Nissim's letter delivered to his son, in preparation for their reunion. Meanwhile he decided to enter a Jewish inn, in order to refresh himself. While there he could perhaps gain some information about his son's circumstances. In those days, the Jewish inns were also frequented by Christians, since for religious reasons the Moslems did not allow Christians to maintain their own hostels, nor were they welcome in Moslem inns. Here, then, Rabbi Yosef met for the first time with Christian travelers from different countries, as well as Christian citizens of Granada itself, who were subject to discrimination and debasing treatment from the Moslem majority.

"We must be grateful," said one Christian citizen, "that the office of vizier is being held by a Jew. He has already abolished many abusive laws against us. In the beginning, any Christian who said something against the Koran or who married a Moslem woman, or who converted a Moslem, was sentenced without fail to death. But now that the Jewish vizier has come to power, the death sentence has been changed to a fine. Even the law forcing us to wear distinguishing dress so that all would know who we were has been abolished by him."

[Shemuel Hanagid

"That is true," agreed another man; "the only decrees that remain against us are those that forbid us to ring churchbells, to eat pork, and to exhibit our cross in public."

"Well," said the first speaker again, "tomorrow we will be given an opportunity to show our gratitude to him."

"What do you mean by this?" Rabbi Yosef asked.

"Do you mean to say you've never heard of Rabbi Shemuel the vizier? Old man, you amaze me! Tomorrow, Rabbi Shmuel's wedding to the daughter of Rabbi Yosef ibn Migash, the Jewish judge, is scheduled to take place, and then the Christian horseriders, the Almugrabis, will perform a splendid rodeo in his honor."

Rabbi Yosef's first impulse was to join the festivities at once and to share his son's joy. On second thought, however, he decided on sending a messenger to inform his son of his arrival. The messenger hurried to the palace to fulfill his mission. When he arrived, the festivities were at their peak. A choir of hundreds was performing a song of praise to the caliph which Rabbi Shemuel had composed some time before, and all the spectators expressed to Khabus their amazement at the talents of his vizier. In the midst of this event a servant entered and informed Rabbi Shemuel that a stranger wished to have several words with him concerning a most important matter.

"Please tell the stranger," replied Rabbi Shemuel,

An Unexpected Wedding Guest]

"that it is difficult for me to attend to other matters at this moment, since I am occupied with the wedding celebration."

"On the contrary," replied the messenger, "he said that it would cause you pleasure if you would allow him to greet you."

The messenger then proceeded to tell Rabbi Shemuel that his father had arrived in Granada. When Rabbi Shemuel heard this, he excused himself from the caliph, in order to personally accompany his father to the palace.

When he arrived at the hotel, he found his father reciting the *Shema*. Rabbi Yosef did not interrupt his prayers and only after having finished did he turn to his son, embracing him soundlessly. Both father and son remembered our Sages' explanation of the patriarch Ya'akov's meeting with his son Yosef, the viceroy of Egypt. The Torah tells us there that Yosef embraced his father, but it does not mention that Ya'akov embraced Yosef. The Sages explain that he was reciting the Shema. Why just at this particular minute? Apparently, when Ya'akov saw his beloved son after many years during which he had believed that his son was dead, he felt his love for his son become overwhelming, and in order to remind himself that all the love in this world must be subjugated to our love for Hakadosh Baruch Hu, he recited the Shema, which commands this in its first verses.

Overcoming his emotion, Rabbi Shemuel now asked

his father to kindly accompany him to the wedding celebrations.

"I cannot come with you, my son," said Rabbi Yosef, "for the troubles of the difficult journey have weakened me. I must rest to regain my strength. You go and delight your guests with your own happiness of heart."

Rabbi Shemuel immediately gave instructions that his father be brought to his home and that his needs be tended to. After the wedding celebration, Rabbi Yosef still had the good fortune to be visited by the respected heads of the city and state who came to congratulate him upon his son's marriage. But his strength waned, he became critically ill, and despite the dedicated care of the best doctors he never regained his strength. Some time later he departed this world and was buried with great honor.

18
the mitzvah feast

It was a joyous day, one year later, in the house of Rabbi Shemuel, grand vizier of Granada. His young wife, Yehudith, had borne him a healthy son, and on this day the infant was to be circumcised, to be brought into the covenant of our forefather Avraham.

The berith milah took place in the large synagogue of Granada and was attended by notables of city and state. Rabbi Yosef ibn Migash, the grandfather, dressed in his most festive clothes, carried in the infant on a sumptuously decorated pillow. Rabbi Shemuel recited the blessing devoutly, with great *kavvanah*, and the large crowd listened in the deep silence which was disturbed only by the wailing of the child. Two hundred wax candles, especially donated by the caliph in honor of the occasion, shed a beautiful light in the hall of the synagogue and filled it with an ethereal glow.

The infant was named after his father's father, Rabbi Yosef, who had died a year earlier. In accordance with custom, however, which provides that a name is not given after a living relative, the baby's name was slightly altered from Yosef, which was also the name of his mother's father, to Yehosef.

[Shemuel Hanagid

After the ceremony had taken place, the guests were invited to gather in a beautifully decorated hall and to join the festive meal, the *se'udath mitzvah*. The Jewish notables sat around the tables together with the poor people of the city who had also been invited to join the meal, as had many Jewish visitors from distant lands who happened to be in Granada at the time. Rabbi Shemuel paid special attention to his needy guests, making it a point to make everyone personally welcome. In addition, he had given instructions to supply suitable clothing for those who lacked it.

Addressing one of the guests who had recently come from Yerushalayim, the Holy City, he said: "Tell me, Rabbi Yehoshua, what is new in Yerushalayim?"

"It is still desolate," replied the man sadly. "Lately the Seljuks and the Egyptian Fatimids threaten us, and a great danger looms over us and over the Christians as well. The Christians have their co-religionists in Germany and France to turn to for armed help, but we have no one to lean on except our Father in heaven. Were it not for the letter that Your Excellency sent to the caliph, thanks to which he granted us special protection, we would have perished already, God forbid. All our brethren in the Holy City are most grateful to you."

"What thanks do I deserve for that? Is it not commanded in the Torah: 'Do not stand idly by your fellow-Jew when he is in danger'? God willing, I will give you another letter to the caliph, and will also make

The Mitzvah Feast]

a contribution for the benefit of the holy yeshivoth in Jerusalem."

Rabbi Yehoshua wished to again express his thanks, but Rabbi Shemuel had already turned to another guest, whose strange garb had aroused the attention of all those present.

"And you, my friend," he asked, "where are you from and what is your business here?"

"My name is Shelomoh ben Yerucham. I, like my father and my grandfather, am one of the notables of the Karaite community in Alexandria in Egypt. Since we conduct our lives by the written Bible text alone, and we heard that here in Spain many important works of Hebrew grammar are available, I was sent here to prepare copies of these books for our community. You, honorable sir, will no doubt be able to help me in this matter."

Not wishing to become involved in a dispute with a Karaite, thereby marring the joyous atmosphere, Rabbi Shemuel replied evasively, and turned to another visitor from abroad.

"And you, Rabbi Klonimos, what is your purpose here?"

"My birthplace, as you may recall, is on the banks of the great river Rhine which divides France and Germany. I live in the region called Lothair, and was sent by our great teacher, Rabbeinu Gershom, Light of the Exile, to show his commentary on the Talmud to Rav Hai Gaon and to obtain his approbation for it.

[Shemuel Hanagid

Since my travels brought me through Spain, I came to this city as well to see your greatness with my own eyes. For you have been fortunate to achieve Torah and temporal success together."

"And how do our brethren fare in Germany and France?"

"There has been a considerable improvement in their status, thank God," replied Rabbi Klonimos. "We have among us one man who is close to the authorities, Rabbi Shimon ben Yitzchak ben Abun, a great Torah scholar and poet as well as a wealthy man, born in France and now living in Mayence. He has succeeded in influencing the emperor, Heinrich the Second, to abolish the decrees of banishment against the Jews. Those already banished have been permitted to return to their places, and even those who were forced to convert have been allowed to return to their Jewish belief. Our great teacher, Rabbeinu Gershom, has issued a *cheirem* (ban of excommunication) against anyone shaming these forcibly-converted Jews in any way."

"Your great rabbi is a true *chasid* (pious person), for he is stringent with his own soul, and at the same time knows how to pity those who were forced to stray from the path. In fact, this calls to mind the commentary of our Sages on the Biblical verse (in the parashah of *Toledoth*): *vayarach eth reiach begadav, vayevarecheihu.* Yitzchak smelled the fragrance of Ya'akov's garments — and blessed him. *Begadav*, his garments,

The Mitzvah Feast]

can also be read as *bogdav*, his traitors: Yitzchak did not withhold his blessing from Ya'akov's descendants though at times there may be amongst them 'traitors,' those forced to convert by cruel decrees, although in their hearts they continue to believe in God and His Torah."

Many other guests were present at that festive meal, from Sicily, from Baghdad, and from Africa, all awaiting Rabbi Shemuel's help and intervention — and each was able to return to his community with his own story of how Rabbi Shemuel had graciously and generously aided him.

The River Darro (now dried) that cuts through Granada. Large Jewish communities lived both to the north and south.

19
a title of esteem

The day after the berith milah of Rabbi Shemuel's son Yehosef, Rabbi Yitzchak de Leon, one of the leaders and dayyanim of the Granada community, invited the Jewish notables who had come from afar, to discuss with them the situation of the Jews in their regions and to deal with their needs.

One of the topics raised by the assembly was the continuing controversy between Rabbi Shemuel and Rabbi Yonah ibn Janach. Rabbi Shemuel had been a disciple of Rabbi Yehudah ben David Chiyuj, the famous grammarian, whose works Rabbi Yonah had also studied. This dispute had already resulted in a whole series of theses and antitheses, of accusations and rebuttals, which centered around the question whether certain Hebrew verbs that have one weak letter (*vav* or *yod*) as the middle letter of their root are actually two-letter verbs, while the major vowel of the first letter comes in place of the middle letter.

All the rabbis and laymen attending the meeting listened to this discussion with the greatest attention. The prevailing preoccupation with Arabic language and literature had sharpened their awareness of the rules governing the Hebrew language. One person, however, listened more intently than the others — an earnest young man, neither robust nor handsome, but dignified nonetheless. After asking permission to take the floor, he said: "Both Rabbi Shemuel and Rabbi Yonah are worthy disciples of Rabbi Yehudah ibn Chiyuj, the great grammarian. Their dispute is of course purely *lesheim shamayim* — to clarify our understanding of the Torah, to illuminate our eyes and to shield them from error. If Rabbi Yehudah's honor is so great in the eyes of Rabbi Shemuel that he refuses to let anyone differ from his view, no-one can call him to task. To me, though, it seems that we in our generation are not yet capable of properly appreciating the towering stature of today's leading personalities and their teaching: only coming generations will be able to do this."

The young man's words convincingly settled the dispute for the assembled guests.

"*Yishar kochacha!*" Rabbi Shemuel cried enthusiastically. "You seem to think that you can hide your identity from me — but you are mistaken! I recognize you well enough, for only you could speak such words. *Shalom* to you, my dear son — Shelomoh ibn Gabirol."

After refreshments had been served, Rabbi Shemuel was called out briefly to another chamber on state business, and Rabbi Yosef ibn Migash, the rosh yeshivah of Granada, requested the floor.

"My teachers and masters," he began, "I wish to

offer a suggestion which has been close to my heart for some time, and now that Jewish leaders from all over the diaspora have assembled here, the time may be ripe to execute the plan."

"What is your plan, Rabbi Yosef?" asked one of the guests.

"I would suggest that we officially proclaim Rabbi Shemuel to be our *Nagid* — the princely representative of Spanish Jewry. In effect, many already call him so, but until now it has only been an unsubstantiated title. In truth, Rabbi Shemuel is the leader not only of Spanish Jewry but of all the Jews in our part of the world. Our brothers from the Maghreb (North Africa), Egypt, Sicily, Babylonia and Eretz Yisrael — all benefit by his intervention with their rulers, and by his generosity. If we officially proclaim him our prince and the representative of all the Jews, his influence will be even more effective, both in relation to the authorities and within our own communities."

"By all means," one of the rabbis concurred. "Except for Rav Nissim Gaon and Rabbeinu Chananel, no-one can compare to him in Torah knowledge. Even Rav Hai Gaon greatly respects him and corresponds with him on Torah subjects."

Another guest added: "Not only that, but he provides for many Torah scholars so that they can devote their time to Torah study. Besides, he has commissioned expert scribes to make many copies of the Tenach, the Mishnah and the Talmud."

A Title of Esteem]

Rabbi Yehoshua, the visitor from Jerusalem, told the assembly that Rabbi Shemuel supplied all the olive oil required to light the lamps of all the synagogues in Jerusalem.

"In short," summarized Rabbi Yosef, "Rabbi Shemuel has acquired four crowns in one: the crown of Torah, the crown of greatness, the crown of the Levites, and the crown of a good name, with good deeds above all. Shall we then officially proclaim Rabbi Shemuel ben Yosef Halevi ibn Nagdilla: the Nagid of the Jews in Exile?"

All of those present gave their full assent to the respected rosh yeshivah's motion, and that very evening a select scholarly delegation presented Rabbi Shemuel with a vellum document, signed by all the Torah leaders in the city, testifying to his appointment by their communities. Rabbi Shemuel thanked them, declaring that he accepted this nomination solely because he hoped thereby to benefit his brethren and to raise the banner of Judaism.

Later that evening, after his guests had dispersed and he remained alone, he contemplated all the strange happenings that had overtaken him from the day of his birth up to the present day — how the Almighty had lifted him up from the depths of poverty to the pinnacle of wealth and influence, until he was the most esteemed personality among his people, and was respected even among gentiles.

Like amora'im before him — who were accustomed

[*Shemuel Hanagid*

to recite *pesukim* (verses) of submissiveness whenever they found it necessary to subdue their hearts and not let arrogance and pride get the better of them — so, too, Rabbi Shemuel began to read passages from the Tenach stressing the futility of human greatness. Then he took out the Book of Koheleth (Ecclesiastes), which teaches the disdain of worldly possessions, and read it late into the night. At length, feeling subdued and insignificant, he went quietly to bed, a prince among men — but a humble one.

An imaginative portrayal of R. Shemuel Hanagid writing to his son from the battlefield.
(diorama at the Beth Hatefutsoth *Museum, Tel Aviv)*

20 Yehosef ben Shemuel

Yehosef, Rabbi Shemuel's son, was born in the year 1035, at the peak of his father's fame as Prince of the Jews in Exile and commander-in-chief of the caliph's armies. This rank of course frequently required Rabbi Shemuel's presence in the field, directing savage battles.

In spite of these overwhelming demands on him, Rabbi Shemuel never neglected the attentions due his home, his wife and children, and his relationship with his son Yehosef was a very special one. He closely watched his development and rejoiced over the progress that Yehosef made in his studies. He was glad to see that his son developed a neat, clear handwriting, so beautiful, in fact, that Rabbi Shemuel entrusted him to copy out some of his poems when he was only six years old. For every poem, he gave his industrious son one coin, a *batil*.

Once when Rabbi Shemuel was away at war, Yehosef sent him a set of poems he had copied, and his father answered with a poem in his praise:

Shemuel Hanagid

> Your pencraft sparkles like sapphires bright
> Your columns as embroidery on a mantle delight,
> Charming the eye like a fig's fruits commencing,
> Fragrant as myrrh, a bride's perfume enhancing.
> Now read much and write, and have your heart set
> On the law of the Ark and of its *kapporet*.
> Persevere ever forward,
> I shall increase your reward.
> Just as a stylus inscribes on a slate,
> So are you engraved in my life and my fate.
> Your love's in my wishes, in my heart's confines,
> My admonition is open — and my love between the lines.

When Yehosef was about seven years old, his uncle Yitzchak suddenly became very ill. In his distress, Rabbi Shemuel decided to consult the famous royal physician Abu Medan, and he rushed off in his carriage to ask him to examine his brother — but by the time they returned, Rabbi Yitzchak had passed away. Rabbi Shemuel was profoundly shaken by the loss of his brother with whom, in humbler times, he had made his footsore way from Cordoba to Malaga. He wrote many laments deploring his brother's death — during the seven days of mourning, at their end, after the first month and after the year of mourning. Later, when he saw other people mourn the deaths of their relatives, he again wept bitterly with them. The laments flowed from his heart into his pen, and only by identifying with the age-old mourning for Zion and Yerushalayim did he find comfort.

Yehosef ben Shemuel]

After the death of his brother Yitzchak, who, during Rabbi Shemuel's frequent absences from home, had been keeping an eye on Yehosef, Rabbi Shemuel's relationship with his son became even closer. He carefully watched over his progress in learning and the development of his noble character. Then, once again, in the month of Nisan 1044, the Nagid had to lead the caliph's armies in battle. Yehosef, who was a mere nine-and-a-half years old at the time, begged his father to let him accompany him. His mother, of course, was not overly keen about this project, but Rabbi Shemuel assured her that this battle was not very far from Granada, and he was confident that he would win it quickly so that he would be home before Pesach. Besides, he wanted to teach Yehosef *hilchoth* Pesach. Finally they were able to convince Yehosef's mother, and so he traveled with his father, in the commander-in-chief's chariot, to the army encampment. At first the only child there was fascinated by the hustle and bustle, the thousands of tents, the husky soldiers and their fleetfooted horses. But soon he became homesick and wanted to write a letter to his mother. His father suggested that he write it in rhyme and even helped him to compose it. This song is preserved for us to enjoy:

> Before I left — I begged to let me go,
> Yet at departure regret began to grow.
> Can a nine-year-old bear going off alone?
> His heart needs be of flint, his feelings like stone.

[Shemuel Hanagid

> My dear ones weep: I'm in a far land!
> Do they know that I'm well, and second-in-command?
> Still, I wish God would end every departure and farewell,
> That no goodbyes in heart and mind should dwell!

One day, on another battlefield, the enemies' soldiers had virtually encircled Rabbi Shemuel's army. He was in a desperate situation and feared that he would not come out of the ensuing battle alive. The night before the decisive fight was to take place, he wrote to Yehosef as in a last will and testament. He enjoined him to fear his Creator and to serve Him with his whole heart, his whole soul and all of his possessions, to learn wisdom and understanding. The Nagid told him to be respectful to his mother and to love and honor his relatives and friends, promising him that thus he would be favored by God and man alike, and would acquire a good name. He also commanded him to be charitable to the poor and needy and to speak to them always in a friendly way, regardless of the circumstances or consequences. He advised him to stay away from high office and to remain humble — the only thing that he should pride himself on, is the greatness of his forefathers. Fortunately, Rabbi Shemuel emerged victorious from this battle too.

He now entrusted Yehosef to take care of his doves, the most efficient means of airmail communication then available. In one of his letters home Rabbi Shemuel wrote him:

Yehosef ben Shemuel]

> By a dove, do send a letter,
> And as it can't talk, it is much better
> To tie a small note to the dove's wing,
> In Hebrew script with carmine ink,
> And when it ascends and aloft it flies
> Send another dove, lest the first one dies
> If in the claws of a hawk, or in a net it should fall;
> The second dove hurries if the first should stall.

In this poem, Rabbi Shmuel proceeded to give an account of his victorious battle: how he succeeded in putting the caliph's enemies to flight and destroyed their armies. He offered up praise to God for His protection and help in winning this battle, and, at the end, he requested Yehosef to have his account read in front of an assembly of the people in Granada.

In this way, Yehosef was able to be a help and comfort to his mother at home when his father was away on the battlefield, while his father entrusted him to carry out his orders, transmit his messages, and copy out his poems, and at the same time depended on him not to neglect his studies.

21 the young poet's visit

Since the days in which Rabbi Shemuel had taught Shelomoh ibn Gabirol in Malaga, much had changed in Shelomoh's life. His parents had both died; his childhood friends had become estranged from him since he had acquired much of his wisdom, especially in the area of philosophy, and their mundane concerns seemed to him petty and inconsequential. Now he had decided to come to Granada to pay his respects to his teacher.

Entering the vizier's mansion, he was ushered into a magnificent anteroom where he had to wait for a while, since Rabbi Shmuel was occupied with a delegation from Toledo. The *objets d'art* on all sides were a delight to the young poet's perceptive eye. Even the religious objects — the silver filigree *mezuzah* case on the doorway, and the finely-wrought Chanukkah lamp that graced a velvet-lined alcove — were executed in exquisite Moorish style, witnesses to the good taste of their aristocratic owner. The next item to catch his attention was the impressive Persian tapestry which divided the anteroom from the inner chamber. He marveled at its beauty. It showed a stylized tree whose branches, spread to both sides, were interpersed with ornamental Hebrew letters. Rabbi Shelomoh was trying to decipher their meaning when suddenly the tapestry moved and Rabbi Shemuel entered the room.

"Shelomoh, my son, is it you indeed? I do not want you to wait outside; please come right in. I only have to give a few more instructions, and after that I wish to hear all about yourself."

On a hint from Rabbi Shemuel, his scribe proceeded to read the gist of the letters in front of him, the uppermost bearing the crest of the Granada caliphs, a sliced pomegranate.

"The Fifteenth District of the country requires a new kadi. The Thirteenth District requires a clerk," read the scribe.

"Do they recommend specific people for these offices?" asked the Nagid.

"They suggest the Arab, Mulabit of the Omayyad family, for the position of kadi and the Arab Mahlal ibn Khani for the clerical position."

"I concur. Next."

"Fifteen Berber families lost all their possessions in the latest Arab uprising and they ask the vizier to provide them with a means of livelihood."

"What was their occupation until now?"

"They were farmers and orchardists."

"Order that they be granted a plot per family from the government lands near Khadikas with sharecropper rights. Also order young fig and olive shoots from

[Shemuel Hanagid

Africa, and let the Berbers try to adapt these trees to our climate. They are to be given three years rent free. Next."

"Here is a problem sent by the Jewish community in Malaga. A band of pirates put up for sale a group of captives who claim that despite their dark skin and uncircumcised condition they are Jews. They are willing to circumcise themselves upon release from bondage. The question arises whether these people are Jewish or are only pretending so that they will be freed. The Jewish community of Malaga wishes to know what to do in this case."

"First of all, they must inquire why the captives were not circumcised in their homeland. Was it due to religious persecution? Besides, it is necessary to know if the price that is demanded for them is reasonable or inflated. After that, we can judge further."

The secretary continued: "The Christian citizens of the land turn to the vizier and request that they be exempted from the head tax as were the Jews."

"This can be granted to them on condition that they pay property taxes like all other citizens. They must guarantee, however, that this revenue brings in at least half of what was collected by the head tax, namely three hundred thousand dinars."

"That is all for today," the secretary said, and left the room with a deep bow.

Turning to Rabbi Shelomoh, the Nagid said: "I am glad to see you in my home, dear Shelomoh. I have heard of your remarkable achievements in Torah and secular knowledge. Your poetic work *Kether Malchuth* is truly superb. I have also seen a copy of another of your poems, which pleased me so much that I have made it a habit to recite it each day before the morning prayers."

Rabbi Shemuel took out a sheet of parchment and read the poem that was inscribed thereon:

> At daybreak I implore Thee,
> Rock and refuge tried,
> Set my prayer before Thee,
> Morning and eventide.
>
> 'Neath Thy greatness shrinking,
> Stand I sore afraid,
> All my secret thinking
> Bare before Thee laid.
>
> O what then can the heart
> And tongue in prayer attain?
> What strength has my spirit to start
> Within me, Thy favor to gain?
>
> Yet since man's praises ringing
> May seem good to Thee,
> I will praise Thee singing
> While Thy breath's in me.

"And now," he continued, "I have heard that several misfortunes have overtaken you, Shelomoh. I would consider it a privilege if you would stay with us

[Shemuel Hanagid

here. I would be glad to provide for you as for my own son."

"I am most grateful for your offer, Rabbi Shemuel," said Rabbi Shelomoh, "although after all that has befallen me, I have more and more to be convinced of the truth of the words of King David, who said with his *ru'ach hakodesh*, 'Do not trust philanthropists, in a person who has no help for himself.' "

"That is true. One must not rely on any mortal. Yet it seems likely, in the normal course of events, that as long as the caliph lives I will be his vizier, for he trusts me implicitly, and he is still in his prime."

Rabbi Shelomoh did not answer Rabbi Shemuel, but merely recited the following *pasuk*: "When his spirit leaves him, he returns to earth. On that day his hopes perish."

At that instant an excited servant burst into the hall breathless, and announced hurriedly, "My master! The caliph wishes you to come immediately. He is dying!"

Rabbi Shemuel was taken aback, but said nothing except for the continuation of the verse Rabbi Shelomoh had quoted: "Fortunate is he whom the God of Ya'akov helps, whose hope is in Hashem, his God."

22
plots and plotters

You will remember Caliph Khabus' ally, prince Zumeir of Elmira, who had aided him several times in his wars. The Elmiran realm bordered Granada to the south and the east, and its capital was situated on a bay of the Mediterranean sea, at the foot of a mountain range, the Sierra de Gador.

At the time of our story, Elmira, like Granada, had reached its golden era in finance and culture. Zumeir's grand vizier was a wealthy Moslem scholar called Mussa ibn Bakana, who was, however, the ruler in name only; the actual reins of the kingdom were in the hands of a Moslem strongman, ibn-Abas, who ruled omnipotently. His wealth was truly unimaginable: conservative estimates placed his property at ten million dinars. His Moorish-style palace was built in royal splendor, with a multitude of servants and slaves to provide every creature comfort. The most famous part of his palace was its huge library which contained four thousand volumes.

Ibn-Abas was considered one of the most educated men in his country, being gifted with a polished literary style and the power of brilliant oratory. He was young and handsome and his family was of noble lineage, claiming ancestry from the ancient families who had been favorites of Muhammad himself. People quipped about him that he had no peer in four things: his literary style, his wealth, his miserliness, and his arrogance.

Indeed his brilliant success fanned his boundless arrogance, which made him many enemies. Once, when visiting Granada together with Zumeir, he made a derogatory remark within earshot of the local nobles: " I have met here only beggars and ignoramuses." From that day on, the citizens of Granada, proud of their riches and scholarship, hated him fiercely.

He even gave expression to his monstrous greed in one of his poems, writing:

> If all men were my slaves,
> I would not be at peace;
> More power my spirit craves,
> Beyond all heaven's reach.

At every opportunity, especially when playing chess, he would say: "Misfortune is always sleeping when it comes to me. It was commanded never to touch me!"

By such foolish statements, he sowed the seeds of his own downfall. He aroused envy and contempt, and one daring poet did not hesitate to express the public's opinion of him. In reaction to ibn-Abas' words, he offered his own sharp retort:

> Providence, now on your side,
> Will not always be fast asleep;
> It will yet turn Misfortune's tide,
> And rouse it from its slumbers so deep.

Being an Arab, ibn-Abas held both Jews and Berbers in contempt, and was strongly opposed to Zumeir's alliance to Khabus, who, as we know, was of Berber extraction, and had a Jewish vizier to boot. In his hatred of Khabus and his vizier, he was of one mind with the Elmiran grand vizier, Mussa ibn Bakana, and together they plotted secretly to depose Rabbi Shemuel. At first they tried to spread slanderous information about him, but without success. Now they decided to foment ill-will and strife between their prince and the caliph of Granada. This plot eventually succeeded.

23 more plots and more plotters

Caliph Khabus had died, and, on his deathbed, had made Rabbi Shemuel swear to have his older son, Badis, succeed him on the caliphate throne.

The people of Granada and its surroundings, however, were sharply divided in their loyalties, and so was the Jewish community. The Arab part of the population was on the side of Badis, while the Berbers tended to side with Khabus' younger son, Balkin. Amongst the Jews, Rabbi Shemuel's followers preferred Badis, while other elements felt that they had more to gain from Balkin's rulership.

Between Granada and Beza there is an extraordinary mountainous region, the Sierra Magina, most of whose inhabitants dwell in caves.

Surveying the view from one of the higher peaks, one thinks that he is seeing a bewitched, petrified village, or some many-turreted, ancient fortress. The hillocks are formed from soft rock which easily lends itself to carving. The inhabitants simply carve themselves apertures into the mounds and shape doors and windows, and occasionally even balconies.

It was nighttime. A ghostly darkness enveloped the

entire area, and in one of the caves a large group of men was assembled. Many torches lit up the interior of the cave, which resembled a large hall. The people within, dressed in dusty white robes, sat brooding on the floor around a mound of earth piled in the center of the cave to serve as a podium. The air inside was stifling.

A fierce-looking Berber got up on the mound and, scrutinizing his audience, began to speak: "Brothers! Caliph Khabus has died, leaving his eldest son, Badis, to succeed to the throne. This will bring disaster on us. We must prevent it! Badis is a profligate, a weak character. He is incapable of responsible rule. Balkin, on the other hand, is intelligent and educated and, what is more, on the side of the Berbers, our side! He is the one worthy of the throne! Let us get rid of Badis!"

A voice shrilled: "Badis means Ismail, the Jewish vizier. They are one and the same!"

"That is the truth," agreed the first speaker. "If we want to depose Badis, we must first depose the Jew Ismail, or Shemuel, or whatever he calls himself. Once we are rid of him, it will not be difficult to depose Badis, too. But before we plan this, I demand an oath of secrecy. Swear, all of you, not to reveal anything about what is being said here!"

"We swear!" echoed wild voices inside the cave.

"Now," continued the speaker, "the majority of the city and the country are in our favor. All Berber notables side with us. Even some Jews sympathize with our side. If Badis does not relinquish his throne willingly, then we will imprison him in his palace and execute him, for the army is with us, too."

"And if there is armed opposition?" asked a voice from the cave.

"We will annihilate them."

"Death to the followers of Badis!" shouted a dozen hoarse voices.

"And what about the Jews?" asked a querulous voice from the darkness.

"Yes, how about you Jews? If you are loyal to your Shemuel, you are our enemies, but if you break your ties with him, we will proceed together with you!"

A Jewish sandal-maker got up and strode to the makeshift podium. He shouted: "Because of that Rabbi Shemuel, I am left without a livelihood. I have been a shoemaker for many years. Many Jews bought new shoes from me and had their old ones repaired. Then a Muslim, Ibrahim, came along and promised them better goods at cheaper prices. So I went to Shemuel to demand justice, for shouldn't one Jew help another? Guess what the vizier said to me."

Total silence reigned in the cave.

And, mimicking the vizier, he continued: "My dear friend, I am sorry to say that I cannot help you in the least. I don't think it fitting in my position as vizier to intervene in such a matter. If he gives better service, let the Jews give their business to him. If I would intervene against the non-Jew without good reason, I would only aggravate the hatred of his countrymen."

"Your claim against the vizier doesn't seem too solid," suggested another voice.

"He doesn't deserve to be called a Jew," insisted the cobbler bitterly. "He hates his people. He must die."

Another Jew, shabbily dressed, went up to the speaker's mound and after much effort succeeded in gaining the floor.

"Tell me, you," he addressed the cobbler, "didn't Rabbi Shemuel give you a handsome sum of money to support yourself, so that you no longer have to work at all?"

"I don't want charity!" the cobbler shouted, his face brick-red. "I want to work for my bread!"

"Yet you took the money," the former retorted with bitter mockery, "and if I know you, you don't mind at all living a life of leisure — without working."

The speaker now turned to the audience and said: "I myself have never benefited even by one penny from Rabbi Shemuel, but I ask you, the Jews assembled here: Who will provide for the needs of hundreds, even thousands of Torah scholars, if not Rabbi Shemuel? Who will provide for the transcription of hundreds of sacred books and their distribution among the scholars?"

The crowd seethed. "Crack his head open!" shouted some angry men.

Another Jew now turned to the Berbers and said: "We Jews are on your side. But we despise bloodshed. Let us try to resolve the matter peacefully."

[Shemuel Hanagid

These words served merely to incite the Berbers. Their eyes sparkled with blood-lust and their faces fully expressed their barbarism.

"If you don't go along with all our decisions, your fate will be like that of Badis and your Rabbi Shemuel — and you'll be the first to go. You won't even live to see the outside of this cave!"

The faces of the Jews paled in fear and confusion. Suddenly a frightful explosion reverberated from the mountains. Terrified and shaken, all the assembled conspirators forgot their rage and hurried outside, looking around to see what had caused the strange sound. But to their astonishment, they could find no source or reason for the unnerving explosion.

Dawn was now breaking in the east. Silently each of the men went his own way.

24
consultation at midnight

Rabbi Shemuel considered it his primary and immediate concern to unite the Jews, for he saw in the division of forces a greater threat than in the rule of Balkin and civil war. The fact that Jews straddled the fence would give an excuse to the victor — whoever he might be — to take revenge on them. The masses likewise would be more than glad to pour out their wrath upon the hapless Jews, whoever the winner.

He now sent one of his trusted disciples to Rabbi Yosef ibn Migash, to Rabbi Yitzchak de Leon, and to Rabbi Nechemiah Ashkapa, inviting them to meet at midnight and consult in secret in one of the historic synagogues of the city. Rabbi Shemuel's eldest son, Yehosef, and Meir Halevi, the oldest son of Rabbi Yosef ibn Migash, would also be present. Yehosef was still a youth, but his father knew that he could be relied on to keep a secret. He therefore invited him in order to train him to understand politics as they are decided upon in the light of the Torah. And indeed, this was an excellent chance for Yehosef to see how great scholars based their joint decisions upon Torah precepts despite their differences of opinion, keeping in mind the common benefit to their people, without personal considerations.

Meir, the son of Rabbi Yosef ibn Migash, somewhat older than Yehosef, was expert in most of the Talmud and considered one of the most promising students in Granada. His father's strength had ebbed with the years, and he needed support in walking.

The six men filed silently into the women's section of the synagogue, being loath to discuss affairs of the world in the synagogue itself. They made no noise, and lit no lamp. Never had the staid arabesques of the old stucco walls been disturbed at this hour by whisperings of such dread moment.

Rabbi Shemuel, the acknowledged leader of Spanish Jewry and one of the greatest Torah authorities of his times, opened the meeting in an undertone: "*Rabbothai*! I have asked you to meet here, in order to try to arrive at some united position concerning the succession to the caliphate. How simple it would be if we could stand aside without mixing into this matter, leaving the *goyim* to settle their dispute by themselves. However, since I have been involved for many years now in political matters, and the well-being of the Jewish community, too, is at stake, we cannot help taking a stand in this issue as well. The worst aspect here is that we are not united in our opinions, for this will give an excuse to the winning side, whichever it may happen to be, to blame the Jews for hàving opposed it. In view of this aspect, I have summoned you

Consultation at Midnight]

here tonight to discuss the problem and to try to find some solution."

Rabbi Yosef ibn Migash rose and said: "Our teacher's words have been spoken truly. How can we best arrive at a unified position? We have to choose between Badis and Balkin, between the Arabs and the Berbers. These two nationalities maintain a very shaky relationship. At the slightest provocation, bloodshed is liable to break out — and we, the Jews, are the buffer between them, caught between the hammer and the anvil.

"That is why I tend to side with Balkin, who is an intelligent person, learned and cultured, who knows how to properly hold the reins of authority, and who will succeed in subduing his opposition. We Jews will be able to depend upon such a friend to defend our rights against our enemies. This is not the case with Badis, who is weak-willed and will not be able to maintain his supremacy over his opponents even if he does come to power, to say nothing of protecting our interests, even if he really wished to."

"My opinion coincides with Rabbi Yosef's," said Rabbi Nechemiah. "I will even add to it. If Balkin comes to power we will gain the favor of the Berbers, which is preferable to that of the Arabs. Who knows when the ancient hatred of the Arabs against the Jews will suddenly flare up? Did not their prophet Muhammad kill twenty-four thousand Jewish souls?"

All present looked expectantly at Rabbi Shemuel,

who now rose to answer Rabbi Yosef and Rabbi Nechemiah:

"Worthy rabbis, you must forgive me if, in the face of the imminent danger to the Jewish community, I cannot be more humble and accept your views, for the sake of peace. However, in these past years, I have become accustomed to the ways of diplomacy and politics in which Hashem has aided me and granted me success in all my plans, as you well know.

"Now Badis is the elder son and thus Khabus' rightful successor to the throne, and as long as we have no sufficient reason to deny him the throne, we cannot oppose him. Even if we are in doubt as to which of the two sons of Khabus is worthier, we are still obligated to favor the elder. In my opinion, however, there is no doubt in the matter. True, Badis is not as capable of ruling as his younger brother, yet for that very reason he should be our choice, for he trusts me as did his late father.

"This will not be true if Balkin rules. He is young and strong and will not tolerate anyone's advice, but will rule as he sees fit. It stands to reason that one of his first acts, if he were to succeed the caliph, would be to depose me, the Jewish vizier, from office, resulting in the ascendance of the anti-Jewish faction to power."

"Still," replied one of the rabbis, "Berber rule is better for us than Arab rule."

"It may look like that, at first sight," replied Rabbi Shemuel, "but Berbers, as their name indicates, are still barbarians, and by their nature wilder and more dangerous than Arabs. In addition to all these reasons, Khabus asked me before his death to support his elder son, and I was forced to promise him this in the presence of several notables. If I do not live up to my word, this will be a *chillul Hashem*, a desecration of God's name, and dangerous as well."

Rabbi Yitzchak de Leon had remained silent during the entire discussion. The youngest of the four, he felt it unseemly to interfere too much. However, at this point he asked permission to address the others, and said: "Our honored rabbis, I see no solution but to try to make peace between the two dissenting brothers. Any other step bodes evil for the Jews. We all agree that either winning side is bound to pour out its wrath and revenge upon the Jews. Even the two together may decide to blame us for the war. We find in the Torah that Moav and Midian, who hated each other, made common cause for the sake of fighting the Jews, when they hired the gentile prophet Bileam to curse them. Although the idea of making peace between the two seems most unlikely, we must try it, come what may. What is your opinion, worthy rabbis?"

Silence reigned for several moments. Finally Rabbi Yosef ibn Migash spoke: "As you say, there is no other way, and we have nothing to lose if we try to reconcile the two sides. Let us do as you have suggested, and may Hashem send you His assistance and put the correct words in your mouth to save our people from danger. I will request ten of my faithful disciples to fast this coming Monday and Thursday and to pray for your success. Is there anything beyond the power of Hashem? The hearts of kings are in His hands; He can bend them to His will."

Dawn was breaking in the east when the six men returned to their respective homes.

Only Rabbi Yitzchak de Leon did not return home. He was overwrought because of the meeting. He knew Balkin personally very well, and realized that the chances for making peace between him and his brother were slim indeed. With a heavy heart, he decided to take a walk outside the city, to view the wonders of Hashem's creation at daybreak after a long night's wakefulness, to quiet his nerves and to attain the peace of mind necessary for *tefillath shacharith*, his morning prayers.

Alone he made his way to one of his orchards on the outskirts of the city. There was a small hut there which usually housed the watchman, but it now stood empty, for the trees were bare and did not require supervision.

Rabbi Yitzchak went inside and sat on a bench, deep in thought, until he was aroused by the sound of lively singing approaching from a distance. Looking up, he saw a group of Slavic shepherds passing by the orchard, singing their merry shepherd songs.

Suddenly the singing stopped. A young Berber passing by flung some curses at them and then spat at them. The insulted shepherds unsheathed their

Consultation at Midnight]

daggers, grabbed the young Berber, and were about to stab him to death.

"Cursed Christians!" the Berber gasped, trying desperately to escape their clutches, "you will regret this."

"Release him instantly!" The thundering command came suddenly from behind. "Whoever dares touch this youth will be held accountable!"

The young shepherds were stunned by the sudden appearance of Rabbi Yitzchak, who, although only in early middle age, had the venerable beard of a sage and, to them, looked like a vision, a metaphysical figure who had suddenly materialized to protect the Berber and save him from their hands. Transfixed, they released their hold on the Berber, who followed in Rabbi Yitzchak's hurried steps.

To his amazement, Rabbi Yitzchak recognized the youth he had just rescued from the shepherds: It was Balkin himself, Badis' brother. Balkin recognized Rabbi Yitzchak, too, and thanked him profusely.

Rabbi Yitzchak was none too happy about this incident. Had he let the Slavic shepherds kill Balkin, he would have solved in one sweep the problem that had occupied him and his friends that past night.

25 the contest for the throne

Returning home after the meeting, Rabbi Shemuel began planning tactics to bring about agreement between the two opposed brothers. First, however, he had to fulfill his duty as vizier and pay his respects to the mourners, hoping at the same time to find out which way the wind was blowing in their attitudes.

He first went to Badis' home. Badis received him most cordially and said to him:

"You were privileged to be at my father's bedside in his last moments, while I was far away. Tell me, how did those last minutes of my father pass?"

"He departed this world with a clear mind," replied Rabbi Shemuel, "envisioning the developments of the future."

"Please tell me more about it."

"The caliph's breath grew short in his last hours; he could hardly speak. However, as soon as he saw me, he seemed to revive. He gathered his newfound strength and spoke to me: 'Shemuel, my faithful vizier — I must be ready to account, to account for my deeds before the Almighty . . . A serious threat from the north

The Contest for the Throne]

hovers over the Arab culture of this entire peninsula... And you, the Jews, will you be able to live in tranquillity under the domination of the northern kingdom? I doubt it... I therefore ask you to support my firstborn son and serve him as you did me. Together, you can prevail.'

"I tried to comfort and encourage him and said: 'Please, my master, do not envision such a dark and forbidding future. You will yet live to rule your kingdom for many years.' But he shook his head and replied sadly: 'No, my dear Shemuel, every rule in this world comes to an end — Persia, Macedonia, Greece, Rome... Only you Jews are eternal. Peace to you.' These were his final words."

Badis was visibly impressed by this. He began pacing the floor, speaking as if to himself: "Maybe my father was right, that our rule, too, will decline. Be that as it may, I am the caliph and the responsibility for the kingdom rests on me, to protect it from its enemies."

"You are not the caliph yet," remarked Rabbi Shemuel.

"What does that mean?" Badis was angry. "Did not my father say before his death that I was to succeed to the throne? Who dares challenge me?"

"Don't you yourself know that? — Your younger brother, your own flesh and blood! I have already investigated the mood throughout the kingdom, and I must confess, to my sorrow, that your chances against your brother Balkin are slim indeed. The Arabs side with you. They value your love of truth and remember to your credit that you took their interests to heart, and used to bring their concerns to your father's attention. However, your blood brothers, the Berbers, who hold the power of the kingdom, side with Balkin. They hate me as well . . ."

Badis scowled and answered: "I have heard that there are Jews, too, who hate you. The situation is very bad. Can we unite all the Arabs and rally them to our side? There are very many. We must go to the Arab masses and find out their views."

"At this very moment," said Rabbi Shemuel, "a meeting is taking place at one of the cafés."

A cunning look appeared in Badis' eyes. He dismissed Rabbi Shemuel and summoned a close aide.

"Let us dress up as farmers, blacken our faces like Moors and go to listen in at the meeting in the cafe next to the mosque. Quickly!"

Before long, the two set out, masquerading as Moorish peasants.

26
a political parable

The function that newspapers serve in our times — as a means of voicing public opinion and criticizing the ills of society, and as a sounding board for political issues — was served then by Arab preachers and kadis, who would appear before the masses and tell them stories hinting at the political issues of the day.

Alongside one of the large mosques of Granada, a large hall had been built to serve as a free kitchen for the poor. This assembly hall, however, had long served as a coffeehouse of sorts where the Arabs would hold their meetings over a cup of black coffee. The walls and pillars were decorated with tablets on which verses from the Koran were inscribed in elaborate, artistic script, and the floor was padded with rugs and mats on which the people sat cross-legged.

On this day, the hall was filled from one end to the other. Utter silence reigned when a dusky sheikh with flashing eyes mounted a small rostrum and slowly began to speak.

"Once there was a great king who had two sons. One son was named Truth; the other — Falsehood."

[Shemuel Hanagid

This opening sentence was enough to arouse the audience. Whispering was heard from all sides.

"The king was always on good terms with Falsehood, who used to flatter him with praises of the country's satisfaction with his rule, of how greatly the country had been enriched by him, and of how superior it was in all aspects due to his wisdom and resourcefulness. The king enjoyed hearing these praises.

"One day Truth wished to gain an audience with his father the king, but Falsehood, the younger brother, objected. 'I know him well,' he said, 'that pessimist, that know-it-all!' Nevertheless, Truth was allowed to enter and said to his father: 'The ministers of your kingdom are unable to perform their duties properly because Falsehood is continually at your side and deafens your ears with his false music. That is why you do not hear the cries of anguish and the echoes of disaster that abound day by day. You never try to understand the wishes of your countrymen. You only want their backs bent under your yoke and their mouths full of your praise. Anyone wanting to tell you the straight truth is banished from your presence like an enemy. You have no real love for your people and do not understand their spirit in the least. Falsehood's influence has spread all over the land. He is the one who permits or prohibits everything in this country.'

"At these words, the king became very angry and banished the audacious son from his sight. Years have passed. The king has died. Let us crown Truth so that the country, relying on Falsehood, will not be doomed entirely."

"Long live King Badis, protector of the kingdom!" the crowd burst into thunderous shouts. "Long live Shemuel, his vizier!" cried others. A tremendous wave of excitement surged through the crowd.

At the back of the hall, Badis whispered to his companion: "Well, now we know that we have the backing of the people here. Let's prepare to fight for our rights." Unnoticed they slipped out, confident in their resolve to stand firm against Balkin and his followers.

27 the power of reproof

That night, everyone sensed that matters were coming to a head: any intervention or peace mission seemed doomed from the start. The tension of impending violence electrified the air.

Setting aside his own weighty causes for anxiety, Rabbi Shemuel went to the beith midrash to teach his regular shi'ur. He opened the gemara to *massechta* (tractate) *Baba Kamma*, and proceeded, as if nothing had happened, to explain the legal question known as *shor shenagach eth haparah*, which concerns the compensation payable for certain damages. His students, knowing full well that during these very hours Rabbi Shemuel's career — even his life — was in the balance, resolved to act like their revered master, and give their undivided attention to their Torah study. It seemed that this night his mind was even keener than usual and his explanations more lucid. It was good to retire a while to the world of learning, and to relish its tranquillity . . .

Suddenly the door flew open, and one of Rabbi Shemuel's agents, who had been sent to reconnoiter the city to size up the developments and report on them,

The Power of Reproof

burst in: "My master," he said breathlessly, "the entire city is seething. Riots and pandemonium rage everywhere. The Berbers have already captured all the fortifications. Many of their men are scattered in hiding places all over the city. They're ready for action!"

"What about the Arabs?" Rabbi Shemuel asked him.

"They, too, have rallied around the sheikh and are ready for battle. If my master desires, the sheikh will send some of his men to protect you."

"Tell the sheikh that for the time being I have no need for his men but that he should do his utmost to protect Badis."

Turning to his students, he continued: "As we were saying before that little interruption, there is an apparent contradiction between these two views on liability for civil damages. However, . . ."

At this moment, a second agent appeared and said excitedly: "The Berbers and Balkin are preparing to attack Badis and murder him. They are also planning to kill you — this very night. The sheikh begs you: flee in disguise!"

At this, there was a crash at the door, and a young, husky, fully-armed soldier burst in, clutching an unsheathed sword in his right hand. The blood drained out of Rabbi Shemuel's face, for he recognized the attacker at once. It was Balkin himself, his arch enemy.

"Hah, Jew!" Balkin exclaimed fiercely. "Do you still want to rule? Here is your just reward!"

He raised his sword, about to plunge it into Rabbi Shemuel's heart.

Suddenly a strong hand struck his upraised arm from behind, and the sword flew out of it.

"Who dared to do that?" he shrieked, whirling around. He was about to pounce on the man standing behind him, but instantly stepped back in confusion: "You?! Why . . . you are the one who saved my life! What are you doing here?"

"It seems I will have to save your life a second time," replied Rabbi Yitzchak evenly. "But this time, it is your immortal life that needs saving. You are about to murder the noblest personage of our generation. You must surely have lost your senses. Do you want his ghost to haunt you day and night? You would find no escape anywhere from his spirit. It would stalk you, and transform your sleep into fearsome nightmares. The sound of his innocent blood would roar in your ears day and night and the sight of his slain body would not leave you forever and ever. His ghost would avenge him, and you would die a horrible, tortured death, and descend into frightful hell. Never again would you find peace — either in this world or the next!"

Balkin was visibly shaken by the thundering voice of Rabbi Yitzchak, who pursued his advantage: "Do you want to establish your rule with abhorrent bloodshed, the murder of innocent people?!"

Obviously Rabbi Yitzchak's reproof was having an effect on Balkin, who was a peace-loving man at heart, and who knew Rabbi Yitzchak well, not only as the savior of his life, but also as being basically not opposed to his rule. He realized that the mob had been goading him to irresponsible actions.

Thoroughly sobered by this experience and by the presence of the calm and venerable sages in the room, he decided on a wiser approach and an attempt to avoid bloodshed — at least for the time being.

Rabbi Shemuel wound up his lesson. At the end, he requested his students to remain and enable him to say the *Birkath Hagomeil,* the blessing of thanksgiving which is said on deliverance from mortal danger. This he did with a full heart, thanking Hashem not only for having delivered him from death, but also for the miraculous way in which the whole Jewish community had been saved from certain violence.

28 Rav Nissim and his disciple

Yehosef, his gifted son, had progressed in his studies and grown in refinement of character. In fact, he was about to surpass his present teachers in the scope and understanding of his Torah learning, yet still found time to continue his work as his father's scribe and secretary.

In the year 1052, when he was seventeen years old, he had occasion to write as follows: "Father received orders to lead the army against the Sevillians, when he heard that I was grievously ill: my life was endangered by a growth. He had once hurried to come and see me. All hope for my recovery was lost, but the Almighty helped me and sent His word to restore my health."

These words appear in *Ben Tehillim*, Item 110, as Yehosef's introduction to a long poem of praise written by his father, explaining the reason which prompted its composition — the Nagid's gratitude to Hashem for his son's recovery. In it he describes his own sudden change of mood, from the exultation of a victor to the anxiety of a father:

> How great my joy! God's saving grace
> Stood by me when in evil case.

Rav Nissim and his Disciple]

> But black clouds marred that sunny day:
> My son on doomèd sickbed lay!
> No time to cringe in doleful anguish:
> I sped to see him, lest he languish!

When Yehosef became stronger, he decided to continue his studies at the yeshivah of the famed Rabbeinu Nissim, even though getting there involved crossing the Straits of Gibraltar, and then journeying across North Africa, 900 miles overland, eastwards to Kairwan in Tunisia. His brothers, Yehudah and Elyasaf, were growing up, and were now able to take over his duties at home as well as those of acting as aide and scribe to their illustrious father. Yehosef wrote a letter of application to Rabbi Nissim, addressing him in the glowing terms customary at that time, as the one

> Whose extensive wisdom is known to all,
> And whose sterling qualities quite enthrall,
> Who shows the way true and straight
> And whose Torah learning is excellent and great.

And the Nagid added a rhymed letter of his own:

> From the day that you became famous in Babylon,
> You were known as the greatest in perception.

Rav Nissim Gaon, who was apparently a *kohein*, was the absolute Torah authority in Kairwan, like his father before him. In fact his word was law in the whole Jewish community of North Africa, and his fame spread beyond it to the whole Jewish world of his time.

Yehosef became a disciple of this great teacher, and

[Shemuel Hanagid

his fame, too, spread in the Torah world, so that when he eventually returned to Spain, many of his brethren in foreign countries came to learn Torah from him. The Ra'avad, Rabbi Avraham ben David of Posquieres, the 12th century Talmudist, is most generous in his praises for him, and writes that he lacked none of the good qualities of his father except for one — that he was not quite as humble.

Rav Nissim Gaon was nevertheless so impressed with Yehosef's profound knowledge and his other wonderful qualities that he consented to give his daughter to him in marriage. Rabbi Shemuel was of course very happy about this match, since the young lady was blessed with all of the modest and charitable character traits he could have wished for, and he arranged for the wedding to take place in great splendor. Grateful that Hashem had granted him, after all the trials of his life, the privilege of witnessing his eldest son's moment of joy, he invited all the poor of the city, and gave ten indigent orphan couples the means to get married at the same time.

When Rav Nissim Gaon arrived in Spain for the wedding, he immediately became the focus of a wide circle of followers who studied Torah under his tutelage. At Rabbi Shemuel's insistence, he consented to remain in Spain for some time, but in due course returned to Kairwan, blissfully ignorant of what lay in store for that center of learning. For soon after his return to Tunisia, in 1057 C.E., Kairwan was sacked by hordes of Arabs who had invaded North Africa from Egypt. Rav Nissim Gaon thus lived to witness the destruction of his own community, and five years later — famous, but saddened — he passed away.

29 prideful provocation

One day when Rabbi Shemuel entered the new caliph's audience room, Badis said to him: "Do you know, Shemuel, my brother's sympathizers are not completely subdued. They are still intent on revenge. I suspect that they are scheming to form an alliance with Zumeir, the caliph of Elmira, and his strongman, ibn-Abas, although I know that you have done your utmost to renew our treaty of non-aggression with them."

"Indeed, it is concerning this very matter that I came to see you, Your Highness. I have just heard that Zumeir and his entourage have crossed the border and are now entering the gates of Granada."

"What?!" shouted Badis angrily. "Without first asking for the right of way?"

Rabbi Shemuel was about to reply, when a commotion reached their ears — shouting, trumpeting, the clattering of horses' hooves and the clashing of swords. Badis and Rabbi Shemuel hurried to the window and saw Elmira's prince accompanied by a splendid royal escort approaching the palace. Badis gnashed his teeth in vexation, deeply insulted by this show of conceit.

"I will have the prince seized and his entourage killed!" he roared.

"With all due respect, Your Highness, I would suggest that you receive the prince with the deference due a ruler and treat the members of his escort graciously. After all, either way they are in our power now."

Rabbi Shemuel had learned this tactic from Elisha, who had advised the King of Yisrael to honor the armies of Aram with a feast and thus make peace with them. As a result of this incident, our Sages taught: "A drink together is more effective than twenty-one battles."

After a moment's hesitation, Badis said: "I will do as you suggest. You can deal with ibn-Abas and I shall presently go to meet Zumeir."

Rabbi Shemuel entered the reception hall that was reserved for foreign ministers. It was a splendid chamber, furnished with the best that Arab craftsmanship had to offer. On exquisitely carved tables stood crystal goblets for cold drinks. The background of dark red wood paneling and the morocco leather chairs was enlivened by green, blue and yellow inlay.

After a few moments, ibn-Abas was ushered in. The two viziers eyed each other, the guest full of the latent hatred he bore against his counterpart. Although he was shorter than Rabbi Shemuel, he tried to give the impression of looking superciliously down at him from an imaginary height. Not waiting for Rabbi Shemuel's invitation to sit down, he chose a soft reclining chair and sat in it, leaving Rabbi Shemuel still standing. Neither did he wait for as much as his host's greeting, but addressed him with a superior air: "I would be curious to know from which strain of nobility you hail, for I only deal with people of the same social stature as myself."

"My lineage," replied Rabbi Shemuel evenly, "is the eldest in the world — and the most honored and exalted. Our lineage is that of distinguished people whose prominent feature is their recognition of the Creator and His uniqueness. We are the rightful descendants of the Patriarch Avraham. The sons of Yishmael," he continued with a penetrating glance at ibn-Abas, "are merely the sons of Hagar, Abraham's handmaiden."

Rabbi Shemuel, who understood human nature well, had succeeded in exposing the weak point of his adversary, who prided himself on his noble ancestry.

"You dog!" Ibn-Abas jumped up from his easy chair, stamping his foot in anger. "I am not prepared to talk with this cursed Jew."

He stormed out of the reception hall and burst into the room where his prince was awaiting Caliph Badis. "We cannot treat the members of this gang like equals," he exclaimed angrily. "They immediately intrude with their arrogance. This Jew has just insulted me in the most impertinent manner...."

Badis, who, thanks to Rabbi Shemuel's influence,

Prideful Provocation]

had remained calm, at that moment entered the room and asked pleasantly: "May I ask what is the meaning of this outburst? Is the meal that I had prepared in your honor lacking something? Please do not hesitate to tell me, and I will immediately command that a more sumptuous spread be brought."

"Your food is quite good," ibn-Abas replied, instead of Zumeir. "What displeases us here is the presence of untamed and stupid people such as your courtiers, specifically your Jewish clerk, Shemuel."

At this boundless effrontery Badis lost his presence of mind, unsheathed his sword and was about to plunge it into ibn-Abas' heart. The involuntary exclamation of alarm of one of his officers stopped him, however. He returned his sword to its sheath, directed a sharp glance toward Zumeir and ibn-Abas and, without another word, left the room.

That evening, a meeting of the cabinet was called, headed by the vizier, Rabbi Shemuel, in order to deal with Zumeir's proposals for a peace treaty. After due deliberation, the cabinet drew up a counterproposal, based on a compromise. The officer who in the morning had cried out in alarm, was entrusted with presenting the proposal to Zumeir and ibn-Abas.

Ibn-Abas measured the young officer with a contemptuous look and after glancing perfunctorily at the text, said: "Go, boy, and tell the one who sent you that we maintain our position and are not prepared to compromise on any point."

[Shemuel Hanagid

"Is that your final answer?" the officer asked bitterly.

"That is the final reply, and if you wish to emply harsher terms than those I used, I have no objections."

The officer returned immediately to the assembled ministers and relayed the haughty reply. At the end he added: "Sirs, this fellow's arrogance is simply too much to bear. We must all unite in order to subdue him, or we will not be able to sit safely in our own homes."

The officer's wrath kindled a like anger among the ministers, who decided to take immediate measures to punish the Elmirans once and for all.

30 ambush in the mountains

After the ministers had left the room, Badis and Rabbi Shemuel remained. "I have a plan," Rabbi Shemuel said. "On their return trip to Elmira, Zumeir and his men have to cross a narrow path between boulders, and afterwards a bridge near El Puenta. Let us destroy the bridge and send our soldiers to seize them at this pass."

"Frankly, for my part, I do not especially hate Zumeir," replied Badis. "I know that he is too much influenced by his vizier, though by nature he is really a good, easy-going man. I have not forgotten the days of our friendship when we were allies and I am still hoping that he might change his attitude to me for the better. I want to warn him of the ambush that awaits him."

"What?! You plot against him secretly — and at the same time warn him against yourself? You will, in effect, be working against yourself!"

"Indeed," Badis said, "but this is the only way that I can be at peace with myself. Listen: I have a Berber officer who once served in the Elmiran army. I will send him to warn Zumeir."

This extraordinary double-dealing aroused Rabbi

[Shemuel Hanagid

Shemuel's apprehension, and the thought struck him that Badis was very much like Achashveirosh, the vacillating king of Persia. "Who knows," he thought to himself, a cold shiver running down his spine, "if one of these days the caliph will not turn against me, despite all I have achieved for the welfare of the state . . ."

Badis did not delay the execution of his wild scheme. Toward evening the Berber officer went in stealth to Zumeir and said: "Believe me, my master, tomorrow you will have a difficult time crossing the mountain pass. I advise you to arise and cross it immediately, before the Granadans attack you."

Zumeir was about to follow the Berber's advice, but ibn-Abas, who was present, said mockingly: "Fear is speaking from his mouth."

"What?!" cried the Berber officer angrily. "You dare to speak thus of me, who have battled on twenty different fronts, while you have not been tested in one? You will see that I am right!"

And he turned around and stalked out angrily.

Behind the tapestry that divided Zumeir from his servants one could hear whisperings. "Do you know why ibn-Abas rejected the Berber officer's advice?"

"Probably because it doesn't appeal to him."

"Fool! Ibn-Abas' most cherished hope is that Zumeir will die in battle with the Granadans so that he can seize the rule of Elmira!"

"And how will he save himself from the Granadan ambush?"

Ambush in the Mountains

"He will flee and proclaim himself ruler of Elmira."

"Tomorrow I will speak to Zumeir about ibn-Abas' scheme."

However, on the morrow it was already too late. When Zumeir, at the head of his soldiers, approached the narrow mountain pass, he suddenly found himself surrounded by Granadan troops. His soldiers were taken by surprise, but he did not lose his wits. He deployed his infantry of five hundred Negroes and his Andalusian troops against the Granadans, and instructed his commanding officer, Hudheil, to storm the enemy with his Slavic horsemen. But just as Hudheil charged, he was pierced by an arrow and fell from his horse. His entire cavalry dispersed in panic; the Negro squadron took the opportunity to defect to the enemy. Thus Zumeir was left with the Andalusian troops, inferior soldiers who now ran for their lives. He had no choice but to flee the battleground. According to Rabbi Shemuel's instructions, the El Puenta bridge had been destroyed and the passes were held by the Granadan soldiers, so the only avenue of escape was to the mountains. But there the Granadan soldiers caught up with them, killing them mercilessly. Among those who died on the steep cliffs was Zumeir.

Ibn-Abas was taken prisoner. The Berber officer who had been sent to warn Zumeir was in charge of the prisoners' stockade. He addressed ibn-Abas as follows: "Do you still think that is was fear alone that made me suggest that you flee? *Now* we'll see who's afraid!"

[Shemuel Hanagid

"Nonsense," retorted ibn-Abas, trying to maintain his usual haughty stance. "I have nothing to fear from Badis. The only thing I am worried about is my precious books. Tell your master to care for my parcels of books; they are worth a fortune."

On that very day, ibn-Abas was brought before Badis. Still laughing, he said: "Well, Your Highness, did I not serve you faithfully by handing over these dogs to you?"

He pointed to the soldiers that had been taken prisoner from the Elmiran army. The Elmiran captives threw angry glances at him, and one officer turned to Badis and cried: "My master, I adjure you by Allah, who this day gave you victory, not to show mercy to this blackguard who brought disaster on our leader. He alone is to blame for our defeat. Ah, if I would be fortunate enough to see his death . . ."

On Badis' orders, ibn-Abas was thrown into the dreaded dungeon of El Hamra, fettered in heavy iron chains. At last, "misfortune had awoken from its sleep" and caught up with ibn-Abas, as the Elmiran poet had foreseen. He knew well that his chances for pardon were nil, for Badis hated and despised him, and Rabbi Shemuel would not recommend mercy for him. Nevertheless, a faint spark of hope still flickered in him, and he offered to pay the sum of thirty thousand dinars in exchange for his freedom. Badis replied that he would consider the offer. There were considerations for and against ibn-Abas' execution. Badis vacillated

Ambush in the Mountains]

between greed for money and desire for revenge, and could not come to a decision. As for Rabbi Shemuel, he knew quite well that if ibn-Abas were freed he would foment riots and wars but, on the other hand, he feared that if he were responsible for the former vizier's execution, his friends would avenge themselves on the Jews in their province. Finally, Rabbi Shemuel recommended to Badis that he sentence ibn-Abas to life-imprisonment. But this advice did not satisfy the caliph, for he would thereby forfeit both the money and the revenge.

One evening, while Badis went horseback-riding, he raised the problem with one of his companions, who said: "It is obvious that if you take the money and set him free, he will foment war against you, and a war will cost you ten times as much as the ransom he is willing to pay you. If I were you, I would have him executed without hesitation."

Influenced by this advice, Badis had the prisoner brought before him.

"Your Highness the caliph," the prisoner begged in a broken voice, "please release me from mental and physical torture."

"Tonight you will be released from your anguish," Badis said in a meaningful tone.

A spark of hope shone in the wretched captive's face, but that was quickly extinguished by the wild laughter that burst forth from Badis. The prisoner flung himself to the ground and began to plead for

[Shemuel Hanagid

mercy in a heartbreaking tone. But in the midst of his sobbing, Badis motioned to one of his bodyguards to stab him in the back. Ibn-Abas was killed on the spot.

Soon the news of the death of the proud ibn-Abas spread all through Granada. The Berbers rejoiced and wanted to celebrate together with the Jews. Rabbi Shemuel, however, did not want anyone to suspect that it was he who was responsible for the death of ibn-Abas, for he feared the Arabs' hatred of the Jews and their revenge. He therefore ruled against any public celebration. Privately, however, he suggested that the Jewish community make a special allocation to buy meat and fish for the poor and his advice was followed. Then, as was his custom on such occasions, in the relief of his heart he composed a song of praise, thanking God for having delivered him from his arch enemy.

Rabbi Shemuel's concern over retribution by ibn-Abas' cronies was justified. One of ibn-Abas' close friends, Aldulla abu-Gafr, tried to incite some of Granada's neighboring princes to avenge the death of Zumeir and ibn-Abas. His instigation was based mainly on arguments against the Jews in general and the Jewish vizier in particular.

One night, as Rabbi Shemuel was sleeping, a voice in his dream breathed the following words:

"Ibn-Abas and his friends are gone. Renew to God your praise. The count, his friend, will be beaten to the ground. Gone will be their wickedness and incitement. May God's name be praised!"

Ambush in the Mountains]

And indeed, a few days later, the news reached Granada that Aldulla abu-Gafr had fallen from his galloping horse and been killed. Thus Rabbi Shemuel was saved once again from the recurring dangers that threatened him in his exalted position.

31
the disputation

Rabbi Shemuel seemed to have entered a period of tranquillity during which he would be able to devote himself to Torah study. He now began to write his great work, *Hilchatha Gavratha*. Of this book only fragments have reached us, but it probably dealt with halachic problems raised in the Talmud.

That year, 4798 (1038 C.E.), saw the death of Rav Hai Gaon, "in history, the last of the Geonim, but the first in rank." He had reached the age of 99, and had retained his physical and mental energies to the end, replying with remarkable vigor to questions submitted to him from all over the Jewish world. According to evidence of his contemporaries, he raised the academic level of the yeshivoth in Babylonia to unprecedented heights. With his death, the glory of Torah in Babylonia declined, and its center of gravity passed to other countries.

The passing of this luminary who had died childless caused deep mourning wherever Jews lived. Rabbi Shemuel bitterly lamented his death in a rhymed eulogy, which is included in his work *Ben Tehillim* (Item 11):

With no dear son to bear his name
In this world was he blessed;
His heirs are students — sons the same,
In all lands east and west.

After the passing of Rav Hai Gaon, it was Rabbi Shemuel Hanagid who became the acknowledged Torah authority, and to him Jewish communities from all over the world now addressed their requests for halachic decisions and for the clarification of difficult Talmudic passages. Fortunately, at this time his political and military duties became less demanding, since Badis, thanks to his astute vizier and commander-in-chief, had by now won supremacy over all his enemies, and had decided for the time being to desist from wars.

The intrigues and instigations against his powerful vizier, however, continued.

One sanctimonious haj (a haj is a Moslem who has made the pilgrimage to Mecca and kissed the Black Stone) resented the fact that Granada's vizier was Jewish, and continually hatched plots against him. He forever sought opportunities to convince Badis that it was a great mistake to entrust his reign to a Jewish vizier. But all his efforts could not influence him. The caliph's trust in his vizier was so firm that he refused to believe anything evil about him. Finally, after much persuasion, the haj succeeded in making the caliph agree to let him try to convince Rabbi Shemuel to convert to Islam.

[Shemuel Hanagid

Rabbi Shemuel was summoned to the caliph, where the haj was waiting for him. Unable to conceal his bitterness at the exalted status of Rabbi Shemuel, the haj began by accusing the caliph himself: "My master the caliph, may he live forever, has made a serious mistake. Even though he could have chosen a vizier from among the believers, he has preferred to choose one from the infidels."

At this, Badis jumped up and cried angrily: "It is not your concern whether I was right to appoint a Jew as a vizier. You can try to make the vizier recognize our prophet and believe in the truth of our religion. And if you do not succeed," he said as an afterthought, "you will be exiled from this land forever!"

The haj then began to quote verses from the Koran that accused the Jews of being moneygrabbers and of having made changes in the Torah. But Rabbi Shemuel, who, because of his involvement in the affairs of a Muslim state, had become familiar with the works of the Yishmaelites in order to be able to reply to them, easily rebutted the arguments of his adversary.

Having exhausted all his arguments based on the Koran, the haj then began to bring arguments based on the Torah itself.

"Is it not written in your Torah," he stated, " 'A prophet from your midst, from among your brethren like me, will be chosen for you by God: heed him'? Whom else can this refer to but to Muhammad our Prophet?"

The Disputation]

"This is a gross misinterpretation of the verse," replied Rabbi Shemuel. "The correct explanation is: 'Just as I (Mosheh) am from your midst, so will God bring forth additional prophets from your midst, one after the other — all from the midst of the Jews.' Your prophet did not come from our midst; he was not in the Holy Land; nor did he continue the prophetic chain of tradition, of one prophet succeeding another.

"Mosheh Rabbeinu," Rabbi Shemuel continued, "was the forerunner of all our prophets and he was believed not only because of all the miracles he performed, but because we ourselves heard him being summoned by God at Mount Sinai to receive the commandments. The Torah of Mosheh is eternal and cannot be exchanged or annulled, God forbid, as it is stated: 'You shall not add to what I have commanded you, and you shall not delete from it.'

"It is further stated, 'The secret things belong to the Lord our God, but what is revealed is for us and our children forever: to fulfill all the words of the Torah.'

"Accordingly," Rabbi Shemuel went on, "if any prophet contradicts the foundations of our sacred Torah, we can never accept his prophecy. Any prophet who denies in any way the commandments of the Torah denies the prophecy of Mosheh Rabbeinu of blessed memory, and that is the sign for us that such a prophet's words are false and his portents only empty magic, for the Torah of Mosheh, in the presence of six hundred thousand adult men, in addition to women and children, was revealed to us so manifestly that it cannot be challenged.

"The fact is that your prophet loved power and pursued pleasure, and selected from our Torah only the things that appealed and made sense to him — much like the man who was proclaimed prophet of the Christians."

Rabbi Shemuel felt somewhat anxious as he let these sharp words against Islam escape his mouth, for he feared Badis' reaction. Badis, however, was impressed by his clear retort. But, because he was unable to publicly acknowledge this, he merely said: "I have never seen a man so wrong present his arguments so capably."

The caliph's reaction thoroughly confused the haj. He tried some other arguments to persuade Rabbi Shemuel, who, however, convincingly refuted all of them.

In the end, the Arab presented his final argument which, to him, appeared irrefutable: "If your faith is the true one, why did Islam capture the majority of the world, rather than Judaism or Christianity? Why does a Moslem mosque stand on the spot where your Temple once stood? Why have thousands of churches been converted to mosques?"

"It cannot be denied that your prophet succeeded in making his belief accepted by a great part of humanity," conceded Rabbi Shemuel. "This power was granted him from heaven, for the Holy One, blessed be

The Disputation]

He, wished that monotheism, the belief in One God, should spread among the nations of the world so that when the true messiah comes, it will be easier for them to accept his faith. As for the Jewish people, our sins have caused us to be exiled from our land and to suffer the yoke of strangers. However, when we return completely to our faith, God in His mercy will again restore His presence to Zion."

When the haj perceived that none of his arguments succeeded in swaying the vizier's belief, he turned to the caliph in despair: "Why, my master the caliph, do you not act as the good, pious caliphs did before you? Why do you not put the Jews in their proper place, as inferior human beings? In the days of the former caliphs, they did not dare blaspheme our religion. They wouldn't have dared to raise their heads, to circulate among our best families and to ride alongside kings and ministers."

To which the caliph replied contemptuously: "With such words of abuse you will not bring Shemuel the vizier to acknowledge our faith. Nor did you succeed in doing this with your verses and quotations. Leave my country this very day, or else your overfed head will decorate my palace gates!"

Gnashing his teeth, the haj turned and left. But before leaving the country, he made sure to prepare a more dangerous adversary for Rabbi Shemuel — an apostate named Abu Sufyan.

Portrait of an imam *(Moslem clergyman) in 18th-century Turkey. As such clerical costume changed very slowly through time and place, quite likely the Moslem who opposed R. Shemuel Hanagid in the disputation looked much like this.*

32 Islam or the sword

Badis now came under even greater pressure to depose his vizier. His courtiers and ministers claimed that a vizier who was a non-believer, an infidel, and who, to make things worse, had even written a sharp polemic against the Koran, could no longer be allowed to be at the head of their state. Badis, who, in spite of his fickleness, still knew where his best interests lay, at first refused to listen to these demands. Nevertheless, when one day Abu Sufyan the apostate came to see the caliph, claiming that he knew of a way to have Rabbi Shemuel accept Islam, Badis gave him his full attention.

"I know of a simple and certain way to get the job done," the apostate said. "You must threaten him with death if he doesn't accept Islam. Then he will be forced to do so, for, in order to preserve his life, a Jew is required to transgress any prohibition of the Torah."

"I was always under the impression that the Jews were ready to give up their life for their Torah," said Badis.

"There are only three major transgressions for which a Jew must rather die than commit them," answered Abu Sufyan, "murder, certain sexual crimes and idolatry. Islam, however, is not considered idolatry by the Jews."

After much hesitation, the caliph finally decided to give in to the pressure of his courtiers, and had Rabbi Shemuel informed that, unless he was prepared to accept the religion of Islam, he would forfeit not only his exalted position, but his very life.

The day on which Abu Sufyan would publicly convert Rabbi Shemuel was designated. This time the debate would be held in a public ceremony. Jews, Arabs and Berbers were permitted to be present at the debate, for which a huge hall with a podium had been especially arranged in the El Hamra fortress. Anyone who could find a place crowded in to gain admittance to witness the spectacle.

The day before the debate, Rabbi Shemuel and his disciples fasted and the whole community recited special prayers, imploring Hashem to stand by Rabbi Shemuel in this trial. In his own prayer Rabbi Shemuel said: "Our God and the God of our fathers, guide the tongues of the messengers of Your people, the House of Yisrael, that they should speak the truth without hesitation, and that they should not utter anything which is contrary to Your will."

On the day of the debate, the streets of Granada were thronged with excited crowds of people. Everywhere, stands had been erected for the sale of cold drinks and fruit to passersby. Groups of people clustered in front of the houses and discussed the coming spectacle.

"At long last," one sheikh said to a group of Arabs standing around him, "the Jew has to pay with his head for all his past arrogance."

This sheikh bore a personal grudge against Rabbi Shemuel, who had once caught him in an act of treason. The surrounding Arabs, however, soon caught his tone and chimed in with his abuse of Rabbi Shemuel and the Jews in general.

Some others, however, held a higher opinion of Rabbi Shemuel. "That Jew," said one scholar who bore a large scroll under his arm, "will know well enough how to extricate himself from danger as he has done many times in the past."

And one kadi who overheard him added: "Better so, for who else would rule the country so efficiently and justly, without an eye to personal considerations?"

Meanwhile, the appointed hour was approaching. The caliph sat on his magnificent crimson-draped throne in the huge arched hall, amid his bedizened courtiers. The galleries were packed to the rafters. Among the spectators, there were many rabbis from the surrounding countries and all the Granadan Jewish notables. In front of the caliph, on a small stage in the center of the hall, stood the two contenders. Rabbi Shemuel's towering height and appearance made a powerful impression on the audience. His face was calm and displayed no emotion at the coming event.

Shemuel Hanagid

The caliph gave the sign for the debate to begin. An important-looking official took a parchment scroll in his hand and began to read aloud: "It is well-known that Shemuel ibn Nagdilla the vizier has composed a polemic against the Koran. The fact that a man who is opposed to the state religion is at the helm of the Granadan government causes harm to our state. Therefore all those who desire the welfare of the state determinedly resolve that the vizier publicly admit and subscribe to the truth of the religion of our prophet. Our master, the caliph, has now decided to hearken to the outcry of his nation against the Jewish vizier, and to condemn him to death unless he accepts Islam. Let the vizier admit today that Muhammad ibn Abdullah is the prophet and messenger of Allah."

The floor was now given to Abu Sufyan, who turned to Rabbi Shemuel and said: "Did you hear, Shemuel, what is demanded of you? I do not need to explain to you that you may acknowledge our faith with a completely clear conscience in order to save your life. You surely know, like me, that Islam is not categorized by your sages as idolatry, for, like the Jews, the believers of Islam do not worship idols and reject any material representation of the Creator. In order to save yourself, you are allowed to embrace our faith and not be killed, for you are commanded to preserve your life. In fact, if you surrender your life without being thus obligated, you will be rendered accountable by heaven!"

Islam or the Sword]

All eyes now turned to Rabbi Shemuel.

"You are mistaken, Abu Sufyan," Rabbi Shemuel said confidently. "According to our sacred Torah, we are obligated *in time of persecution* to surrender our lives even for the smallest commandment. It is obvious that just such a situation of religious persecution is about to develop against Jewry at large. In such a case, the Talmud explains, one must sacrifice one's life and not even submit to a change in the color of one's shoelaces. That is, if Jews are accustomed to tying their shoes with black laces while the gentiles use red ones, and the latter try to impose their red laces on the Jews, the Jews must sacrifice their lives in time of persecution even for such an insignificant custom as this, which symbolizes an extra measure of modesty."

"There is no basis for your contention that this is a time of persecution," Abu Sufyan retorted. "No-one will prevent the Jews of Granada from believing in the faith of Mosheh and fulfilling its commandments publicly. This situation concerns only one single man who is required to convert to Islam for purely political reasons, for the good of the country. Your arguments are therefore null and void, Shemuel."

"Even if we assume that your are right and that this is not the beginning of a period of persecution, I am anyway not permitted to do what you are demanding of me. Our rabbis, the Sages of the Talmud, taught us that if a Jew is required to transgress any commandment of the Torah in public, that is, in the presence of ten Jews, he must rather sacrifice his life for the sanctity of God, and not commit the transgression. Moreover, accepting your prophet means rejecting the entire Torah and the prophecy of Mosheh our Teacher, of blessed memory, who told us that the Torah is eternal, and this, without a doubt, would be a form of idolatry.

"Besides," he continued, "in many places in the Talmud and the Midrash we find instances of self-sacrifice, even to uphold other commandments. Rabbi Akiva and Rabbi Chanina ben Teradyon sacrificed their lives for Torah study. Daniel risked his life for the mitzvah of prayer. In view of this, some of our great sages in France and Germany rule that we are permitted to sacrifice our lives for the sake of keeping any commandment, and that this does not constitute a transgression of the obligation of self-preservation."

Abu Sufyan's face showed signs of consternation: the chances for converting Rabbi Shemuel were dwindling.

"Such a situation is clearly the case here," continued Rabbi Shemuel. "Imagine if I would, God forbid, do as you tell me. I would thereby cause a spectacular, unprecedented *chillul Hashem*, a desecration of God's Name. For generations on end, I would be a prime example of the betrayal of Judaism, just as we today point to Yochanan the High Priest, who, after a lifetime of faithful service in the Temple, became a *Tzeduki* (a member of the dissenting Sadducee sect) at the age of eighty! Under the circumstances, I feel that it is clear without any doubt that I must sanctify God's Name."

"You are a stubborn and obstinate sinner," Abu Sufyan shouted loudly, as if by raising his voice he could compensate for his lack of intellectual acumen. "You merely have a blind hatred for our religion: that is why you will not concede to our demands. And I am sure you would not do so even privately," he added, "even if there were no public desecration of God's Name involved."

"I have already stated," Rabbi Shemuel replied, "that the argument of the public desecration of God's Name is not my only deterrent to acknowledging Islam, although by itself it is compelling. For one thing, accepting the prophecy of Muhammad constitutes a rejection of the holy Torah of Mosheh and of his prophecy — and this is tantamount to idolatry. For another, in the words of our Sages, 'the hour demands it,' meaning that the social climate makes it necessary. If this doesn't satisfy you," Rabbi Shemuel continued, "I can add that several of our scholars maintain that Islam is indeed a form of idolatry, for to this day you are not altogether free from idolatrous customs. For instance, your ritual involving the Black Stone in Mecca is nothing but a relic of the worship of the idol Mercury, which consisted of stone-throwing. To be sure, the majority of our Sages do not consider Islam an idolatrous religion; still it cannot be called unadulterated monotheism."

[Shemuel Hanagid

Abu Sufyan suddenly felt like a soldier on the battlefield stripped of ammunition: he saw that Rabbi Shemuel was unafraid and was fully prepared to give up his life rather than accept Islam. He now increased his accusations against Judaism in general: "You maliciously label us, the Mohammedans, *minim*, meaning heretics, and pray for our destruction three times a day, when you say your prayers: 'And all the *minim* shall perish in a moment.' You also say, 'The Kingdom of Wickedness shall speedily be uprooted,' no doubt meaning us. Thus you curse the believers of our prophet — and the caliph himself — every single day!"

"You are mistaken as to our definition of heresy," replied Rabbi Shemuel. "Heretics are those who deny the basic tenets of our faith, especially the existence of God, or regard Him as a physical being, or else deny that He is One. The latter are called *minim* after the philosopher Miani. Similarly, the disciples of Jesus the Nazarene are also termed *minim* in the Talmud, for they obscured the tenets of the Torah and perverted the words of the living God by their false interpretations. The believers of Islam, on the other hand, are not *minim* at all. As for the Kingdom of Wickedness, this refers only to the government of Rome because they, in their wickedness, destroyed our Holy Temple. What is more, the prayers which you refer to cannot possibly concern Islam, for they preceded the founding of the Islamic religion by hundreds of years!

"Regarding our master, the caliph, and the

Islam or the Sword]

caliphate itself," Rabbi Shemuel continued, now turning to Badis, "surely you see for yourself that I devote my life to the interests of our country. How can you possibly accuse us of praying for its downfall? Quite the contrary, we always pray for its prosperity and welfare."

Deeply impressed by the vizier's words, the caliph rose from his throne, approached Rabbi Shemuel, kissed him on the forehead, and said: "Remain true to the religion of your fathers, and I will continue to have complete faith in you. But Abu Sufyan," he continued, looking at the apostate, "who intimidated you with the fear of death, will be thrown into the darkest of my dungeons, where he can contemplate which religion is the true one, till the end of his wretched days."

The audience burst into thunderous applause, and shouts of approval filled the hall. The news quickly spread throughout the city and throngs of Jews crowded near the entrance. As soon as Rabbi Shemuel emerged, he was lifted on the shoulders of the crowd to the sound of proud cheering.

When he returned home and found himself alone, he retired to the stillness of his study. Such a sublime moment as this must not be marred! He took down his favorite old tomes, and once again browsed over the Biblical passages which speak of humility, in order to overcome any feelings of pride that might have found their way into his heart.

33
poetic pranks

In Rabbi Shemuel's summer palace in Elmira, young Rabbi Shelomoh ibn Gabirol found respite from the trials and tribulations that had beset him since early youth. In this palace, which was furnished in excellent taste and offered every comfort — truly a small-scale El Hamra — Rabbi Shelomoh was able to dedicate himself to the study of Torah without distractions. The spectacular scenery, merging the delicate beauty of the nearby green hills with the wild grandeur of sheer cliffs in the distance, offered inspiration to Rabbi Shelomoh's poetic soul.

Occasionally, he received friends who came to discuss Torah matters, but in the main he kept to himself and let his proud and demanding spirit pursue its search for the profound truths of life. Here he wrote his important philosophical treatise *Mekor Chayyim* (Well of Life), which on its way through the centuries became a source of knowledge even to gentiles (it was translated into Latin), and here he unfolded his great poetic genius that we can still see and enjoy from the beautiful poetic *piyyutim* he composed, which remain our treasured heritage to this day in our daily and

Poetic Pranks]

holiday prayers. Thus Rabbi Shelomoh lived a life of peace and tranquillity in Rabbi Shemuel's home — until dissension occurred between these two great men.

Rabbi Shemuel was accustomed to inviting many guests for the Purim se'udah, at which he indulged freely in wine and revealed his generous heart and noble spirit. One Purim, some of his friends decided to test the measure of his prowess in Talmud. Although he always tried to hide the extent of his scholarship, unless there was need to evince it, he nevertheless gave in to their efforts at loosening his tongue at the Purim meal. It became evident that not only did he know all of the Mishnah and the Talmud by heart, but also Sifri, Sifra, Tosefta and Talmud Yerushalmi. No matter what he was asked, he displayed an amazing expertise. The peak of his guests' amazement came when the "examiner" erred several times and the "examinee" had to correct him, which he did by composing a short poem on the spot.

That Purim, as he did each year, Rabbi Shemuel prepared a lavish feast. He personally graced the head of the table, while to his right sat a young guest whose striking black beard flowed down his chest, and whose intelligent eyes bespoke a deep inner awe of Hashem. His expression had an ethereal quality about it, every gesture bespoke nobility and, despite his youth, his appearance commanded awe. This esteemed guest was Rabbi Bachya the Dayyan, destined to become famous decades later for his classic work, originally written

[Shemuel Hanagid

in Arabic, *Chovoth Halevavoth* (Duties of the Heart). This work — in which Rabbeinu Bachya clarified those obligations incumbent upon a person's "heart" rather than his body, such as faith, trust and love of Hashem — was the first of its kind. Similar treatises, called works of *musar* and *yir'ath shamayim*, appeared only later. Rabbeinu Bachya was a chasid, a pious man, who practiced what he preached, and his chasiduth was scrupulously weighed out on the scales of his intelligence.

Seated at the head of the table were also Rabbi Shelomoh ibn Gabirol and Rabbi Yehosef, the eldest son of Rabbi Shemuel. The se'udah was held in the large courtyard in front of the summer palace, for the rooms inside, spacious as they were, could not accommodate all the guests. In the center of the courtyard played a magnificent fountain, whose droplets sparkled with the hues of the rainbow as they showered down upon a marble floor.

As the wine flowed freely, Rabbi Shemuel began to compose impromptu poems in perfect rhyme and meter about the colors dancing among the gushing waters, about the small fireplace which stood before him, and then on to other subjects around the courtyard.

The waiters served ruddy apples, placing a bowl of the choicest ones before Rabbi Shemuel. This was the signal for a fresh poem — this time in Arabic — about apples. The next moment, faces were focused on Rabbeinu Bachya, who launched into a simultaneous translation in metered Hebrew. Rabbi Shemuel did not lag, but proceeded to retranslate his own verse into differently-metered Hebrew — and continued from there to compose another thirteen verses on the same subject, each time with different words.

Once those poets had demonstrated their virtuosity in verse, Rabbi Shelomoh ibn Gabirol took a turn at contributing some rhymes of his own. But here something unpleasant occurred. Rabbi Shelomoh, whose spirits were high with wine, began to praise the pleasant weather, which was neither cold nor hot; mentioning the cold, he included an impolite reference to the "lack of warmth" in Rabbi Shemuel's verses. This sting, which was intended as a passing joke, left a grating impression on the gathering, for it was not fitting to speak thus about the leading figure — the Nagid — of the generation. The only one to react immediately, however, was Rabbi Yehosef, the Nagid's son, who felt it was his duty to object to the slight against his father. He called out to Rabbi Shelomoh: "Stop right there!"

The poet paled. An oppressive silence reigned, and an unpleasant atmosphere chilled all those present. But Rabbeinu Bachya quickly saved the situation by saying, "My friends! Rabbi Shelomoh certainly did not intend to purposely insult Rabbi Shemuel's honor, but since he did come out with words which aroused resentment from the Nagid's son and his admirers, it is only fitting that he appease our Nagid in public."

Statue of R. Shelomoh ibn Gabirol (by the American sculptor Reed Armstrong) erected by the municipal council in Malaga, Spain.

Poetic Pranks]

Rabbi Shelomoh, much relieved, immediately accepted Rabbeinu Bachya's suggestion and composed on the spot a long poem in praise of Rabbi Shemuel's greatness.

The banquet continued uneventfully afterwards, although Rabbi Shemuel's disciples still harbored resentment toward Rabbi Shelomoh, feeling that the wine had made him show his true negative feelings toward the great man. As our Sages testify, "A person is truly recognized by three things: his pocket, his goblet, and his anger." And even though Rabbi Shemuel objected to his students' continuing desire to uphold their teacher's honor, nevertheless they did not stop their barbed remarks, which strained the relationship between the two great personalities. Rabbi Shelomoh now began to feel uncomfortable in his surroundings.

A few days later, he entered Rabbi Shemuel's study in order to speak openly about the incident at the Purim banquet. He wished to ask him to influence his students to remove from their hearts the resentment they bore toward him. As he found Rabbi Shemuel in conversation with Rabbeinu Bachya, who had come to take his leave, he did not think that this was the proper occasion to speak about the purpose of his visit and, with due apologies, turned to leave. Rabbi Shemuel, however, invited him to stay. "Have you heard," he asked his two guests, "that Rav Nissim Gaon intends to return to his academy in Kairwan? I have tried to persuade him to remain here, but with no success."

[Shemuel Hanagid

"What is his reason?" Rabbi Shelomoh asked.

"He is dissatisfied with the attitude of the students here. He feels that they indulge too much in Greek philosophy, a practice which does not befit *beney Torah*."

"And what of it," Rabbi Shelomoh wondered, "as long as they do not accept those conclusions of Plato and Aristotle which differ from our sacred Torah? Their conclusions are based on logic and rhetoric, and as long as they do not contradict the Torah, surely we may accept them."

Rabbi Shemuel rose as if to reply and, removing a parchment letter from his drawer, handed it to Rabbi Shelomoh and said: "Read this *teshuvah* (responsum to a halachic inquiry) which I received from Rav Hai Gaon when I asked his opinion on this subject. He wrote this letter a short while before his death, and sent it to me via Rav Nissim Gaon."

Rabbi Shelomoh took the letter and read it aloud: ". . . The way to restore and improve the body and the soul, and to make a man's conduct upright and proper, is to engage in the study of Mishnah and Talmud. This is good for Jewry at large, for the study of Torah is of benefit to one's own self and to other wise scholars, and is likewise of value to the unlearned, since it draws them to the pathways of the mitzvoth and the Torah. If, however, a man turns his heart away and occupies himself with those subjects that you have mentioned, he will thus lose the reverent fear of Heaven, and be harmed thereby, until he casts off entirely all the words of the Torah. It thus occurs that people's good sense becomes distorted until they can even come to abandon their regular prayers and other mitzvoth. Those Jews, however, who devote themselves to Torah and the reverent fear of Heaven, find as a result that they can lead the entire mass of ordinary people likewise to the awe of Heaven and to true *teshuvah*, to repentance without any doubts or misgivings, and will thus not create any doubts about the Holy One, blessed be He. Now, should those who busy themselves with these subjects tell you that they are on the right highway and that by this study they gain a knowledge of the Creator, do not pay attention to them. Know that in truth they are lying to you. You will not find the reverent fear of God, or alacrity to serve Him, or humility, purity or holiness in any person but those who occupy themselves with the study of Mishnah and Talmud."

Rabbeinu Bachya listened intently to Rav Hai Gaon's unequivocal statement on the basic educational problem of their times, and with the words, "Let us hope that these guidelines will be followed by the new generation," he took his leave of his host and Rabbi Shelomoh.

34
preparing for the end

Gradually, Badis' unsteady hold on his government began to be felt. In the long run, the genius of his vizier could not save the caliphate from the effects of the fickle character and decadent nature of its ruler. Eventually Muhadir, the powerful prince of Seville, began to erode Badis' rule by attacking the small Berber provinces surrounding Granada, subduing these one by one to his own rule.

When Badis learned of the fate of his allies, he started to lament, and rent his garments. When he heard that, in the wake of Muhadir's victories, all the Arab citizens of the city of Ronada had risen up to revolt against their Berber masters, dark forebodings crept into his heart and depressed his spirit even more. Would his own Arab subjects join their kinsfolk in the neighboring states and threaten his throne and his life? The thought threw him into a nightmare of fear. Night and day he paced his room back and forth, dreading that hidden somewhere in the darkness, murder was lurking. Often he would burst into wild tantrums for no apparent reason, cursing and berating everyone within earshot. At other times, he would lapse into a deep melancholy and sit for hours in bleak silence, staring straight ahead as if he found no reason or purpose to life.

His delusion of fear so much obsessed him that eventually he saw an assassin in every Arab and concluded that as long as there were Arabs in his kingdom, he could not regard his life as safe. He therefore decided to destroy the Arabs one and all, and actually intended to carry out this project one Friday while all the Arabs were assembled in their mosque — an ideal opportunity. He summoned Rabbi Shemuel to come immediately, in order to charge him with the execution of this plan.

Rabbi Shemuel was alarmed at the caliph's appearance. His face was ashen and his expression frightful. His flaming eyes were ringed by black circles. His fleshy hands continually trembled with fear.

"We must kill every last Arab in this country!" he said in a rasping voice, and went on to reveal his diabolical plan to Rabbi Shemuel. "Whether you agree or not," Badis added with special emphasis, "I have so decided. I will execute this plan."

Rabbi Shemuel was appalled at the caliph's words. He could only try delaying tactics, but these were of no avail. Badis insisted: "I have thought of nothing else for weeks. My decision stands." And, with the cunning of a madman, he added: "And don't think you can get away through your subterranean tunnel, my friend, for I am having it watched!"

Rabbi Shemuel had indeed been thinking of this way of escape that he had prepared for himself and his family and was filled with consternation that Badis had discovered it. However, he did not let his face show the slightest sign of fear and, as if he had not heard the remark, advised Badis: "Let us assume that you succeed. Do you really think that the Arabs of the neighboring countries will do nothing about such a horrible act? Surely they will retaliate and declare a *jihad* (a holy war) against you. Countless forces will rise against you and wield their fanatic swords against your kingdom!"

The fixed expression of Badis' face did not change. He waved his hand deprecatingly and said, "I will manage this without you. Just don't talk about it."

After Rabbi Shemuel left the palace, the caliph summoned several of his trusted men and instructed them to execute his plan on the following Friday. He told them to concentrate the army with its weaponry not far from the mosque under the pretense of a military parade.

Rabbi Shemuel was in a quandary. Either way his life was in danger: if he revealed the plan, Badis would make short work of him — and his Jewish brethren would be victimized, too. If he did not reveal it and the dreadful slaughter were to be carried out, it was he who would be held responsible for it, and he and the Jews could expect Arab revenge.

In the end he decided to send several respected men

to the Arab notables to advise them not to assemble at the mosque on the coming Friday, warning them that their lives would be in danger. The Arabs followed his advice and so it happened that on the appointed day only very few people were present in the mosque.

When Badis saw that his plan had failed, he immediately sent for Rabbi Shemuel. Knowing that he was going to face a murderer on the rampage, his wife attempted to dissuade him from going, begging him to flee for his life. But Rabbi Shemuel refused, saying: "Of course I would prefer to spend the remainder of my life in peace in the Holy Land and devote myself to Torah study. However, even if I escape now, I will be apprehended within three days at the most." And, ruefully, he added: "Even my underground tunnel cannot help me now. Still, with the help of Hashem, perhaps Badis will change his mind again and have mercy on me."

"Go in peace," said his wife. "Hashem will surely guard you from all evil in the merit of your good deeds."

Rabbi Shemuel retired for a short while to his study, where he contemplated several Biblical passages that deal with *bitachon* (trust in Hashem), recited the *vidduy*, the final confession of mortal man, and entrusted his soul into the hands of his Father in heaven. By the time he stood before the caliph, he was completely tranquil. He had balanced all of his worldly accounts and turned his thoughts to his Creator, to whom he was now prepared to return his soul in purity.

[Shemuel Hanagid

Badis received him with a scowl, and growled: "It is you who revealed the secret!"

"Who told you that I was the one who revealed your secret?" Rabbi Shemuel replied evenly. "It is easy enough to understand that the Arabs did not come to the mosque, seeing all your troops assembled nearby. After all, there is no war on, so it was not difficult to guess the true intentions behind that military parade. Besides, Your Highness, instead of being angry, you should thank heaven for preventing you from executing your scheme. Consider, if the Arabs wished to rebel against you, would they not have rushed to do so the moment they learned what you were planning to do to them? You can see for yourself that they did not even lift a finger against you, because they have no evil intentions against you."

Rabbi Shemuel's calm, assured words greatly surprised Badis. While he hesitated whether to accept this explanation or not, a Berber sheikh who was present turned the balance in Rabbi Shemuel's favor. "The vizier's words are logical and we must thank Allah for preventing this massacre."

"Thank you, Charvonah," said Rabbi Shemuel to the sheikh.

"What name did you just call me?" the sheikh wondered. "Don't you know my name is Ahmed ibn-Akba?"

"I know," Rabbi Shemuel replied, "but you remind me of a man who once saved the Jews by saying the

[202

Preparing for the End]

right thing at the right time. And he is remembered favorably to this very day, just as you will be."

"Indeed, I see that I have erred," said Badis. "I will not scheme against the Arabs in my kingdom again. The people of Seville, however, will feel the power of my hand."

Some time later Badis set out to engage the prince of Seville in battle and subdued him.

Rabbi Shemuel then became the vizier of a vast and mighty empire. His health declined, however, as a result of the latest incidents, especially because of his supreme efforts in the war against Seville. As his strength no longer sufficed to manage all the affairs of the kingdom, he gradually initiated his son Yehosef into the administration of various governmental departments. Rabbi Yehosef resembled his father in everything — in wisdom, in piety, and even in his knowledge of Hebrew. The caliph was satisfied with his work and relied upon his judgment in everything he did.

A short while afterward, Rabbi Shemuel became seriously ill. The entire Jewish community of Granada prayed for his recovery. Speedy messengers were sent to all the neighboring communities to arouse the public to pray for mercy for their leader. His disciples fasted. But, after several days, the angels bested the mortals and captured the great man's soul. Fully conscious to the last minute, he recited the verses of Shema, accepting, for the last time, *ol malchuth shamayim*, subservience to the Kingdom of heaven. Finally, with the word "echad," he breathed his last.

Rabbi Yehosef was appointed vizier in place of his father, and the Jewish community, as well, accepted him as the successor of the Nagid in the realm of Torah.

On the ninth of Teveth, 4826 (1066 C.E.), a Shabbath, there was a great Berber uprising in which 1,500 Jewish families were killed in Granada. The victims included Rabbi Yehosef and the heads of the Granada community, as well as many Jews from foreign lands who had been drawn there to study Torah. All of Rabbi Shemuel's precious manuscripts were plundered and dispersed throughout the world — some of them coming to light, at least in fragmentary form, after centuries, and others remaining lost forever to posterity.

A man, however, is not a manuscript. The lifework of Rabbi Shemuel cannot be plundered, and his memory continues to come to light, even after nine centuries — as the man who passed on the Torah from the last generation of the geonim to the succeeding generations of the rabbanan; and as the man who excelled in an extraordinary combination of careers during his lifetime — as a statesman, military commander, scholar and poet.

In our national gallery of outstanding personages, the Nagid stands as a truly unique figure. His achievements remain an imperishable part of our history.

GLOSSARY

Note: Since italic type amid regular (roman) type tends to be distracting, it was thought best to keep words and phrases in italic to a minimum. For this reason, transliterated Hebrew words, etc., have been set in italic only at their first appearance, with a translation or explanation added in parentheses. Subsequently such words and phrases appear in regular (roman) type, except where a long Hebrew phrase might seem strange in roman type.

aggadic: relating to the moralistic, poetic or narrative (i.e. non-halachic) passages of the Talmud
alluf: lecturer in a *methivta*, a Babylonian Torah academy
amora: Talmudic authority cited in the Gemara, third to fifth centuries C.E.
av beith din: senior judge of a rabbinical court
avodah: divine service, specifically in the Temple
Baba Kamma: a tractate of the Babylonian Talmud
Bavli: Babylonian
beith din: rabbinical court
beith hamikdash: the Temple in Jerusalem
beith midrash: communal study house
beney tarbitza: part-time students in Babylonian adult-education Torah seminars
beney Torah: Torah students
Bereishith: Genesis
berith milah: (covenant of the) circumcision
bimah: synagogue rostrum for public reading of the Torah
Birkath Hagomeil: prayer of thanksgiving after deliverance from danger
chacham: sage
Chanukkah: festival commemorating the Maccabees' re-dedication of the second *beith hamikdash*
chasid: pious man
chasiduth: piety

[*Glossary*

Chathan Torah: worshiper honored with the public reading of the concluding passage of the Torah
cheirem: ban of excommunicaton
chillul Hashem: desecration of the divine Name
Chummash: the Pentateuch (Five Books of Moses)
dayyan: judge in rabbinical court
Elul: month of spiritual stocktaking preceding New Year
Eretz Yisrael: the Land of Israel
Gan Eiden: the Garden of Eden; Paradise
gaon (pl. *geonim*): literally, excellency; the title of the head of one of the Babylonian academies after the Talmudic period, from the sixth to the eleventh centuries C.E.
Gemara: the major part of the Talmud, which discusses the *Mishnah*
Gittin: a tractate of the Babylonian Talmud
goyim: literally, nations; gentiles
Hakadosh Baruch Hu: the Holy One, blessed bé He
halachah: the body of Torah laws; also, any one such law
    halachic: pertaining to the halachah
    hilchoth: the laws of (whatever subject)
Hanagid: see *Nagid*
Hanassi: title of various Jewish communal heads, notably Rabbi Yehudah Hanassi, the editor of the *Mishnah*
Hashem: literally, the Name; i.e., God
    Hashem yithbarach: God, blessed be He
hashkafah: philosophy of life
hatzaddik: the righteous one
Iyyar: second month of the Hebrew calendar
jihad (Arabic): holy war
kadi (Arabic): judge in Muslim religious court
kapporeth: cover of the Holy Ark in the Temple
Karaites: dissident Jewish sect which denied the authenticity of the Oral Tradition of the Sages
kavvanah: devout concentration in prayer
Keneseth Yisrael: the community of Israel
kohein: priest

kohein gadol: high priest
Koheleth: the Biblical Book of Ecclesiastes
lesheim shamayim: for the sake of Heaven; i.e. altruistically
massechta: tractate of the Talmud
mechayyeh hameithim: (blessing praising Him) Who resurrects the dead
Megillath Esther: the biblical book (or scroll) of Esther
methivta: Torah academy in Babylonia
mezuzah: tiny scroll affixed to doorpost
Midrash: aggadic (see above) commentaries on the Bible
mikveh: bath for ritual immersion
Mishley: the biblical book of Proverbs
Mishnah: (pl. *mishnayoth*): the basic legal passages in the Talmud which are discussed by the *Gemara*
mitzvah (pl. *mitzvoth*): commandment; religious precept
musar: ethics
Nagid: prince; title of the head of medieval Jewish communities in Muslim countries
Nisan: the first month of the Hebrew calendar
parashah: a weekly portion of the Torah read in the synagogue
Pesach: Passover
pesukim (pl. of *pasuk*): biblical verses
pidyon shevuyim: ransom of captives
piyyut: liturgical poem
rabbanan sevora'ey: post-Talmudic Sages
Rabbeinu (literally: our master): title of a distinguished rabbi
Rabbothai: my masters (form of address)
reishey kallah: heads of the Talmudic academies
rishonim: the early medieval legal authorities
rosh yeshivah (pl. *roshey yeshivah*): head of a yeshivah
ru'ach hakodesh: divine inspiration
se'udah: meal;
    se'udath mitzvah: festive repast accompanying certain *mitzvoth*

[Glossary

shacharith: the morning prayers
shalom aleichem: peace be with you (greeting)
Shechinah: the Divine Presence
Shema: (the first word of) the Jew's affirmation of faith (Devarim 6:4)
shi'ur: lesson, lecture
talmid chacham: sage
Talmud (Babylonian): the basic compendium of Jewish law and moral teachings, compiled at the end of the fifth century C.E., and comprising the *Mishnah* and *Gemara*
techiyyath hameithim: resurrection of the dead
tefillah: prayer
Tehillim: the biblical book of Psalms
Tenach: the 24 books of the Bible
teshuvah: (a) repentance; (b) a rabbinic responsum to a halachic query
Torah shebe'al peh: the Oral Law (comprising the Talmud, Midrash, etc.)
Torah shebichthav: the Written Law (i.e., the books of the Bible)
Tzeduki: Sadducee; member of a certain dissenting sect in the period of the second *beith hamikdash*
yarchey kallah: month-long seminars in Babylonia for extramural adult students
Yerushalmi: Jerusalemite; name given to the Palestinian Talmud
yeshivah (pl. *yeshivoth*): Talmudic academy
yir'ath shamayim: fear or awe of heaven
yishar kochacha: the more power to you (congratulatory greeting)
Yishuv: the Jewish community in Eretz Yisrael
Yoma: a tractate of the Babylonian Talmud
Yom Kippur: the Day of Atonement